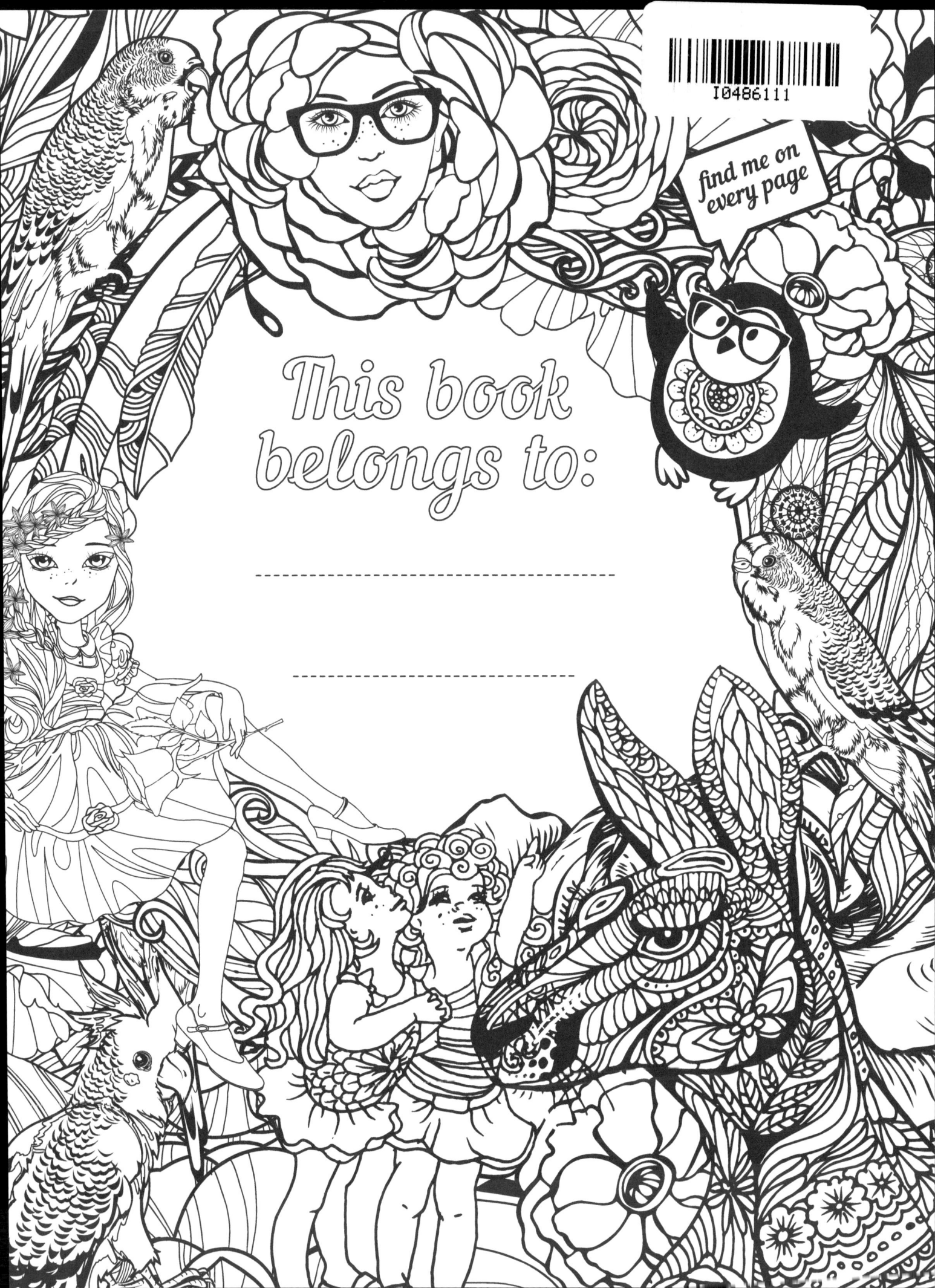

This book
belongs to:

_____

_____

find me on
every page

I0486111

some hints & tips from percy...

Colours...

❀ If you're having trouble choosing a colour why not 'Go in Blind Folded"?
Just pick up a color and go for it. Let the spirit of spontaneity take over.

❀ Try looking to nature, She always has fantastic colour combinations! Be inspired by Plants, Flowers, Stones, Shells, Birds, Butterflies and Animals. I love the different tones and shades of colour found in the ocean and sky. Especially a sunset. Many create Pintrest boards purely for colour inspiration.

❀ Experiment with warm and cool colours. You can create some amazing effects using complimentary and contrasting colour combinations.

Tried and tested...

❀ Put a piece of paper inbetween the pages if coloring with Markers (especially Sharpies or Copics) they do bleed through a lot. This will protect the artwork on the following page.

❀ Test out your colours out on the page provided, Markers can behave differently on different papers.

❀ Try to build up colour gradually if you are using pencils. Do this by only applying light pressure on the pencil.

❀ Be sure you keep your pencil nice and sharp when tackling those tight spaces and lines. Marker users may wish to swap over to a fine liner or gel pen for these areas.

❀ Water colour pencils can create some amazing effects. Use them like regular pencils, then wash water over an outlined area to create an instant watercolour effect.

Rules: There are no rules!

❀ The great thing about colouring is that there are no rules, Your imagination is free to colour and create in which ever way that pleases you in the moment. It's amazing to see variations of the same illustration all coloured in so uniquely. Markers, Gel pens, Charcoal, Oil pastels, Pencils, Paint, inside the lines, outside the lines, Block colour, Shading or adding patterns and doodles, sparkles & embellishments... anything goes!

Relax to the Max...

❀ Health research has shown that colouring in promotes wellbeing by calming the mind, focusing your senses and promoting creativity and a sense of satisfaction in creating something beautiful.

Why not:
Fix yourself your favourite drink, light a scented candle or two,
Listen to you favourite music while loosing yourself in:
Percy and the Colouring Wonderland.

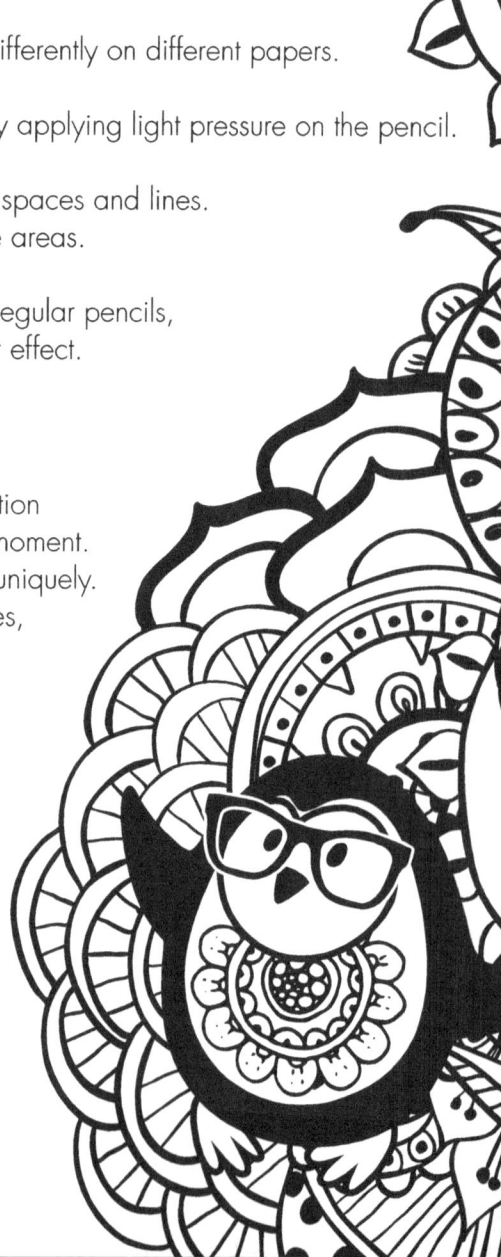

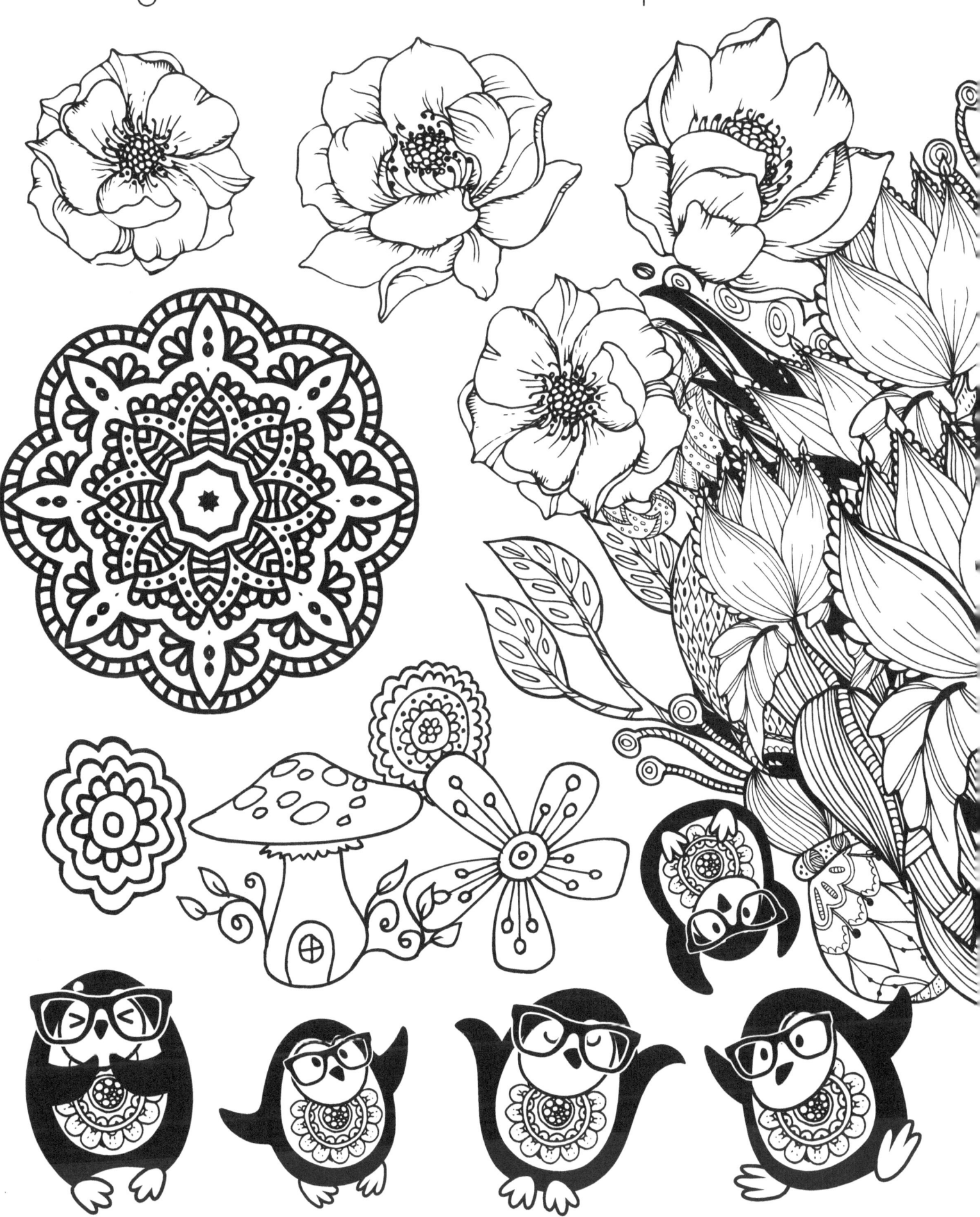

PERCY THE LITTLE PENGUIN

When you find yourself lost, find your way home...

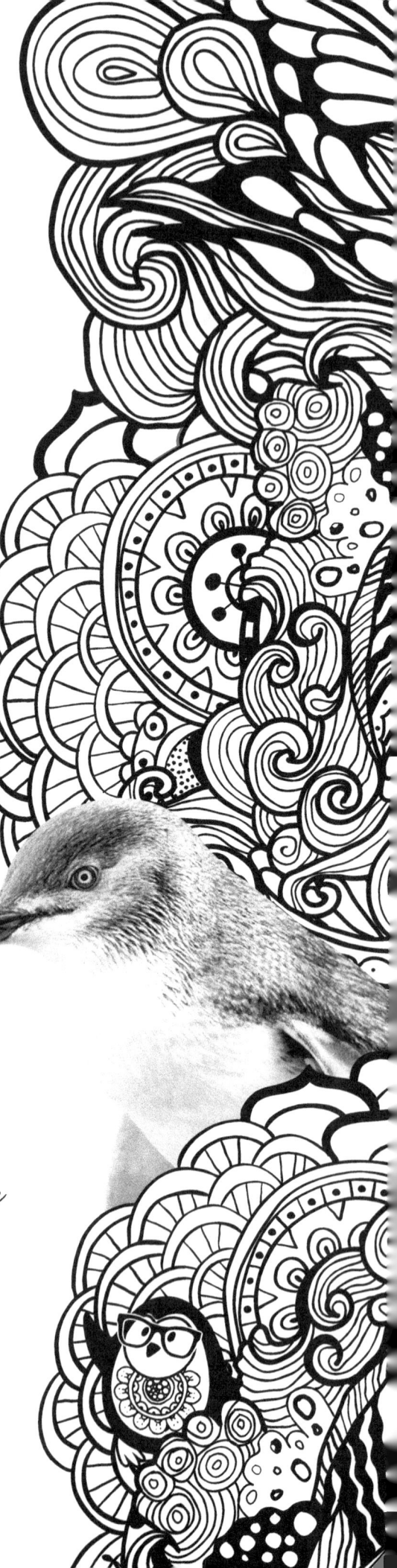

The story of Percy, The inspiration behind this book...

I found Percy while walking on my local beach in Torquay, Australia. He wasn't in great shape, but luckily the team at the Jirrahlinga Wildlife Sanctuary (Barwon Heads) were able to rehabilatate Percy, as they do for hundreds of distressed wildlife each year.

Percy is a 'Little Penguin' also known as a 'Fairy Penguin' He doesn't live in Torquay and had obviously lost his way, I imagined the sights and experiences Percy might have encountered on his journey far from home. That was the beginning of some of these illustrations. Little did I know that years later they would be transformed into a beautiful adult colouring book!

Enjoy finding Percy on each page, just as I did on the beach on that chilly winter's day so long ago.

Narelle Craven
Artist & Illustrator

A percentage of proceeds of this book will be donated to help other Penguins

JIRRAHLINGA
WILDLIFE SANCTUARY

Play with colours & techniques here...

Illustrator: Narelle Craven
and her inspiration for this book

Narelle has worked for Roxy, Quiksilver and Ripcurl in fashion design after completing a degree in Graphic Design/Multimedia. She launched her Graphic Design Studio 'Logozoo' in 2006 creating unique brands and logos for businesses worldwide. View her portfolio at: www.logozoo.com.au

Living in the small coastal town of Torquay (Victoria, Australia) Narelle finds inspiration from the surrounding environment. The local beach and bushland often feature in her illustrations.

A percentage of proceeds from this book go towards the rehabilitation of injured animals at the Jirralingah Wildlife Sanctuary (Barwon Heads). Narelle has found creative ways to illustrate some of the sponsored animals. If you look closely you will see them within the pages of this book.

You may also notice that little girls often feature in her illustrations, sometimes as fairies or fantastical beings. Her three creative and energetic daughters, Aged 5, 3 and 2 are often the inspiration for these images. As well as the imaginary and fantasy worlds that are dreamed up by children or children's books.

The last major theme for inspiration throughout this book is all things vintage. Narelle loves to up-cycle and re-use furniture and items from a time gone by. This influence can be seen the designs, patterns and items throughout these artworks which have been inspired by her own collection.

Narelle's illustrations are also available as colouring-in Greeting Cards and Large Posters.

Shop online:
www.colourofcalm.com.au

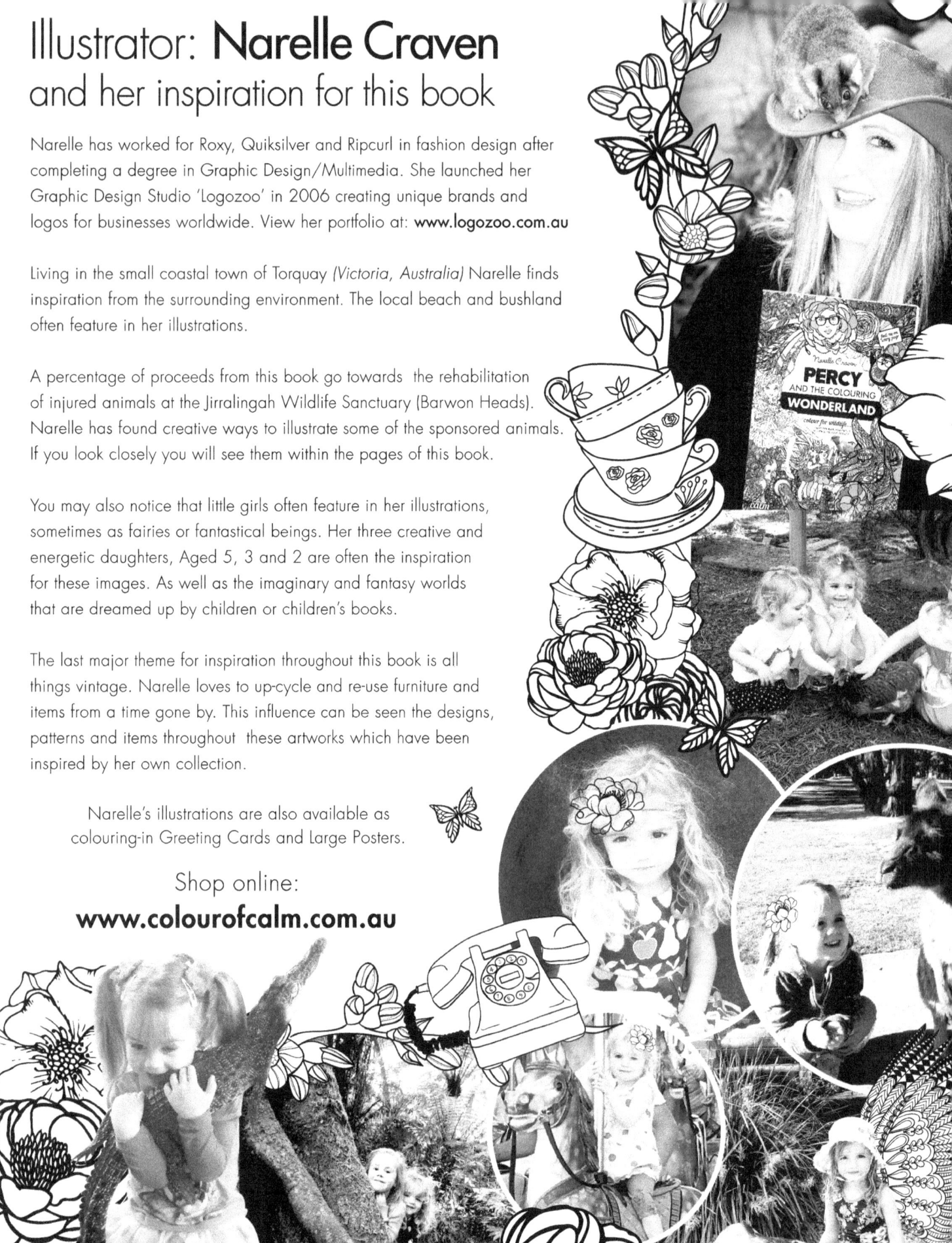

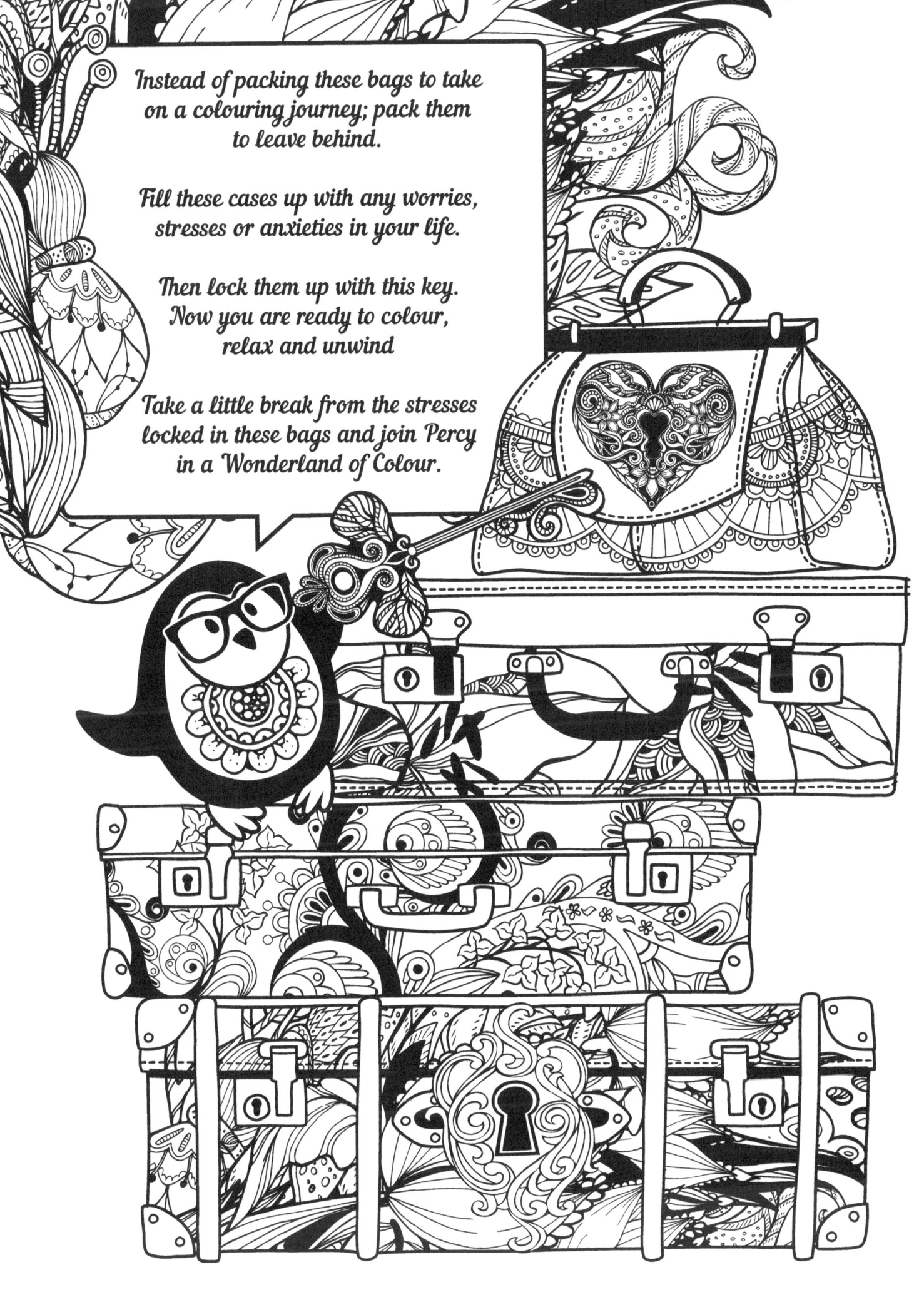

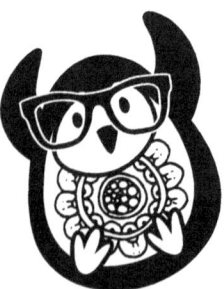

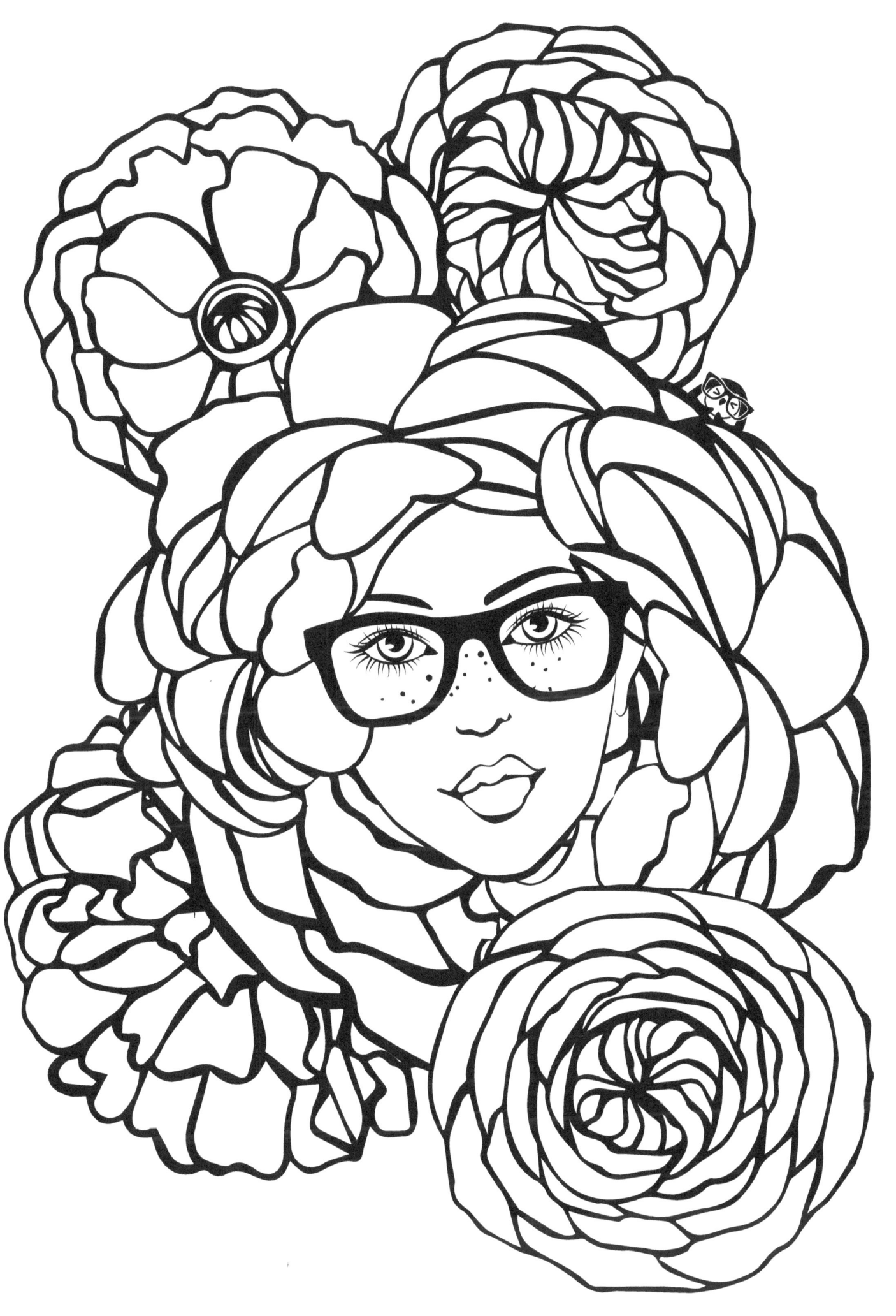

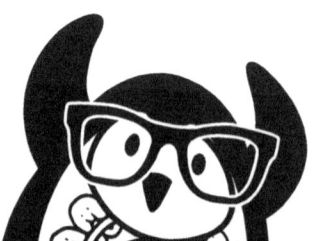

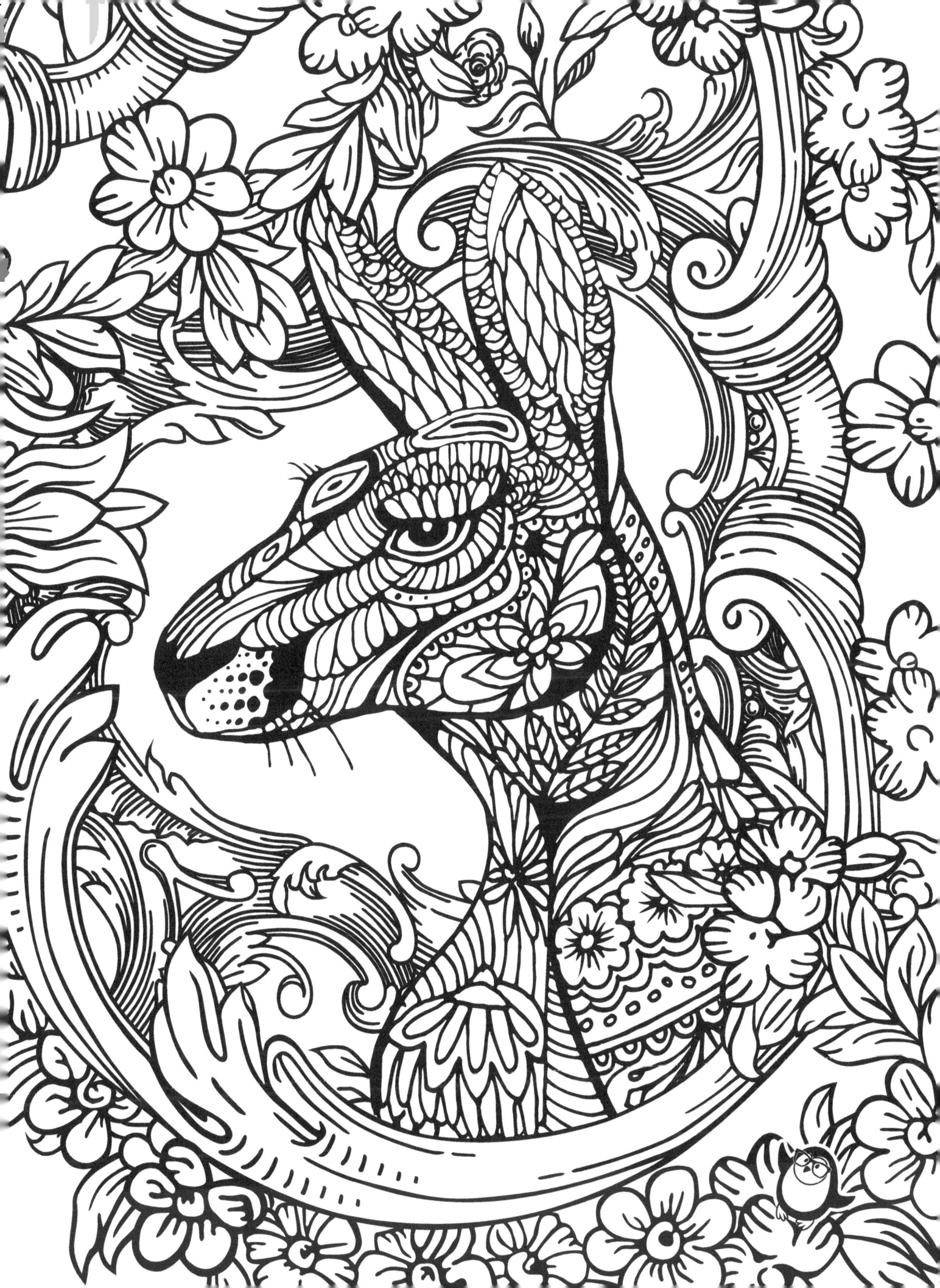

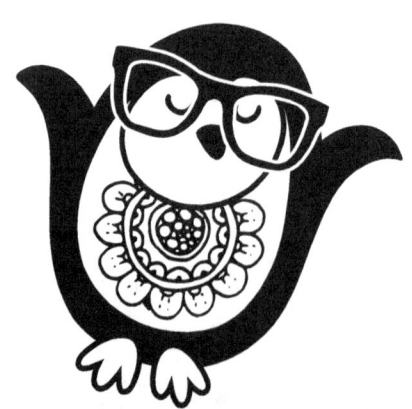

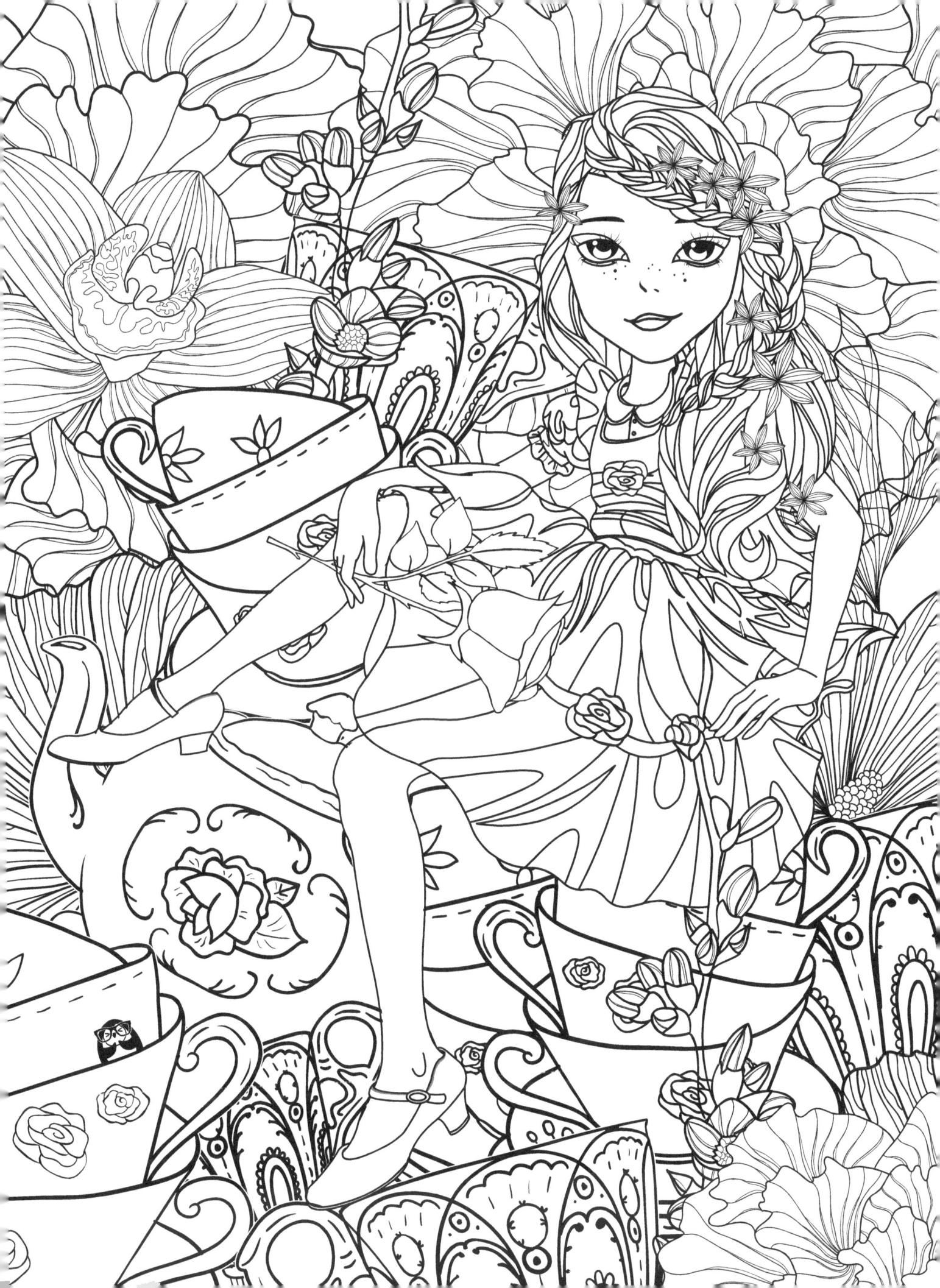

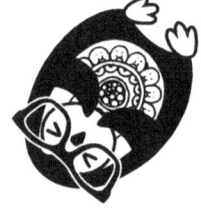

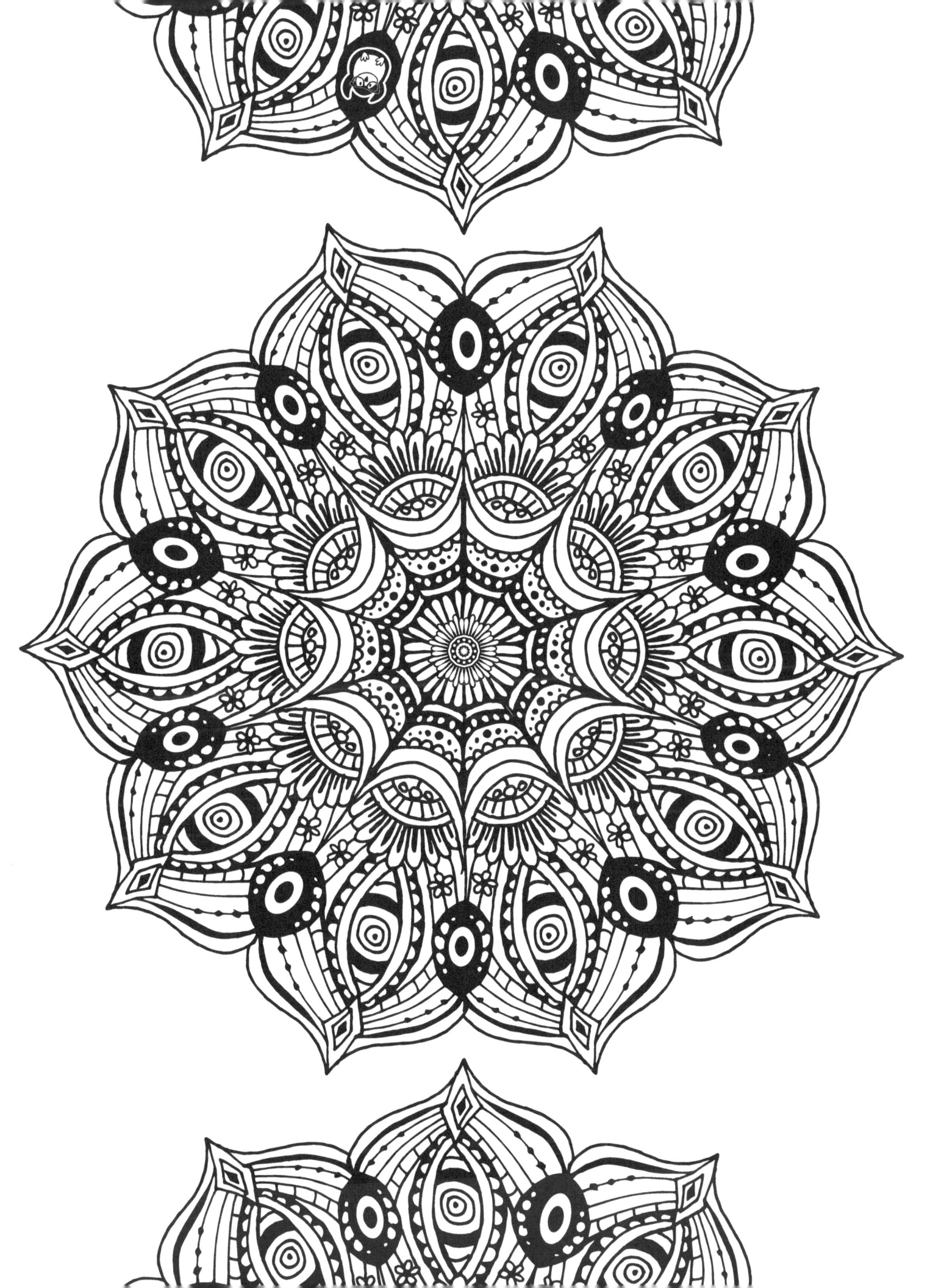

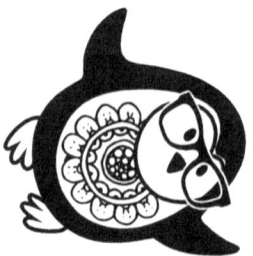

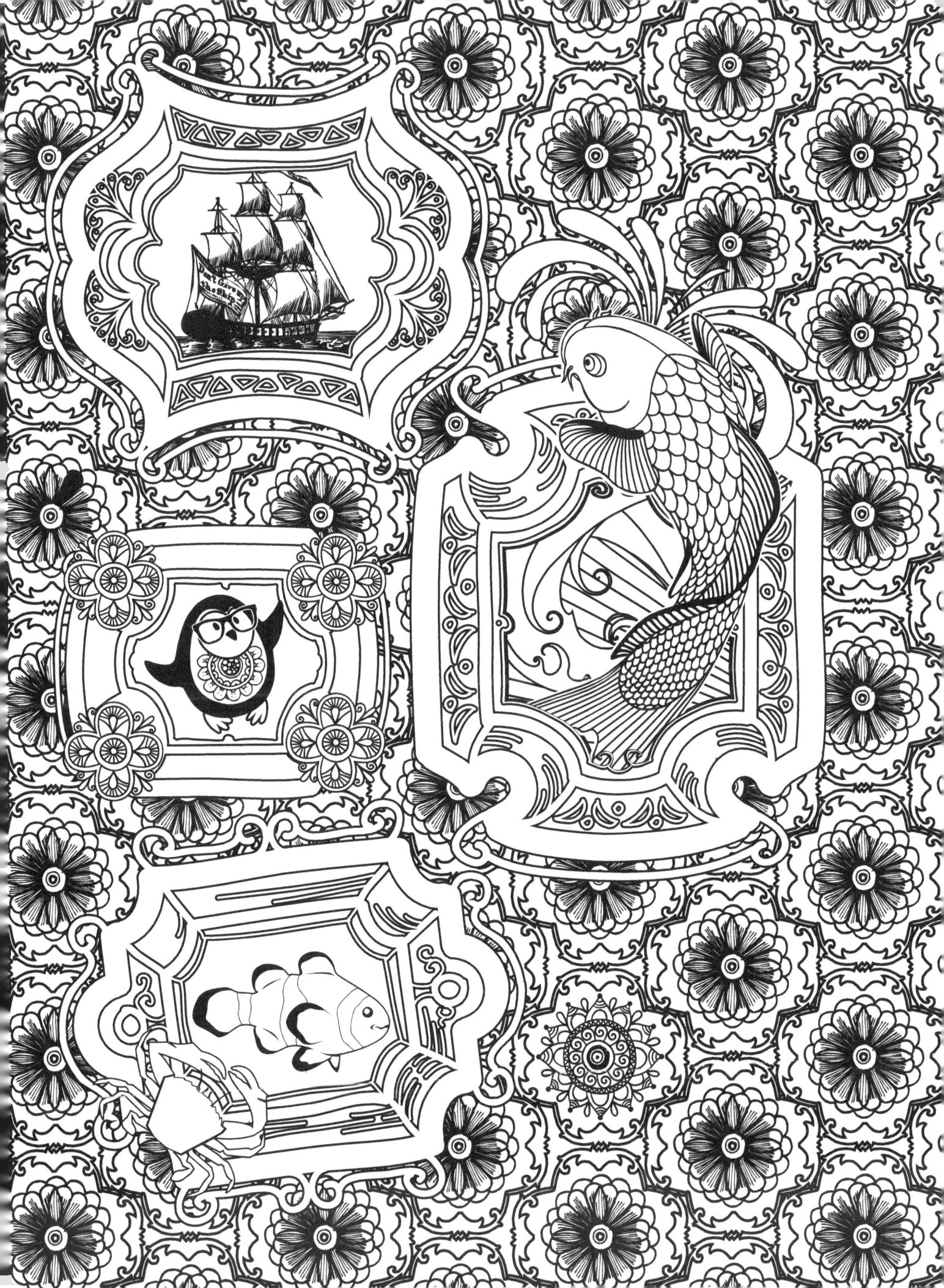

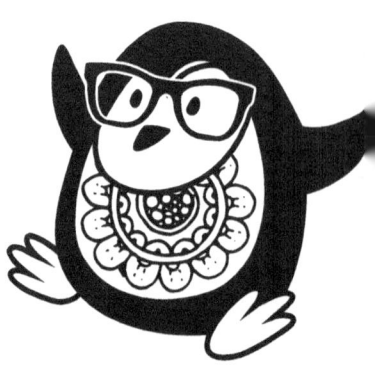

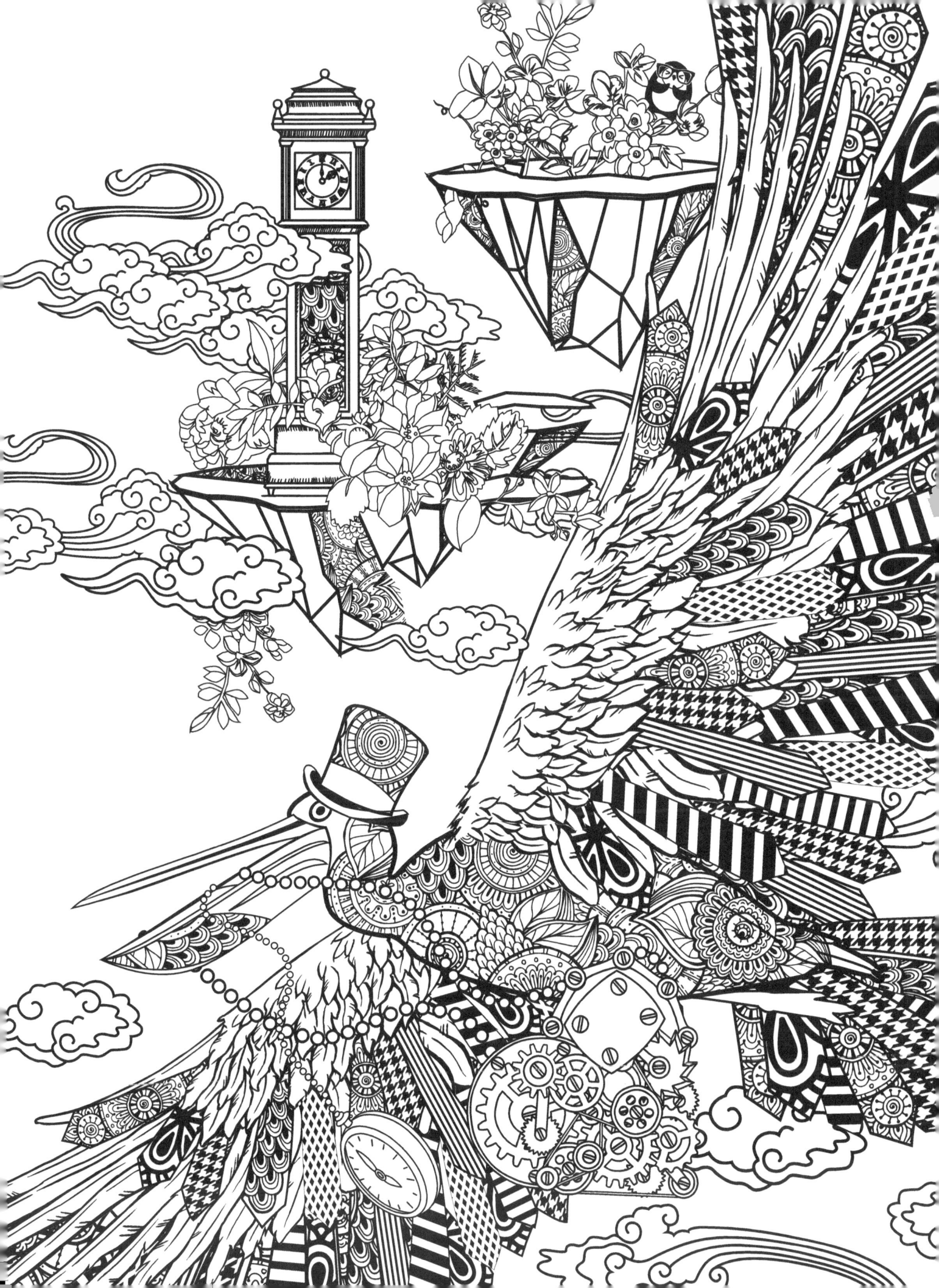

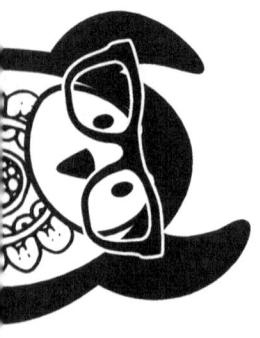

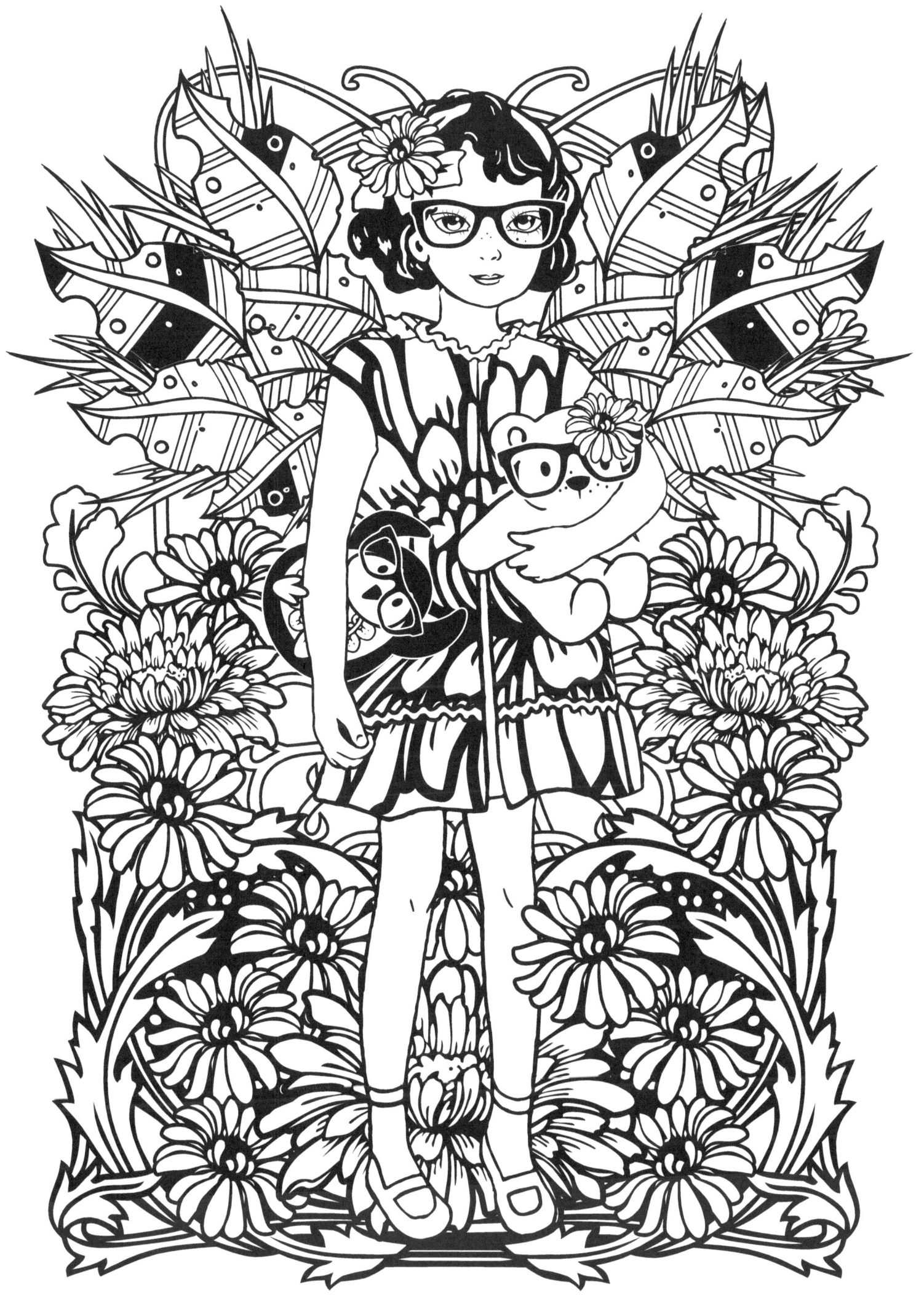

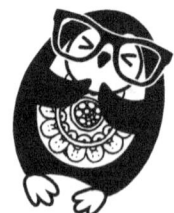

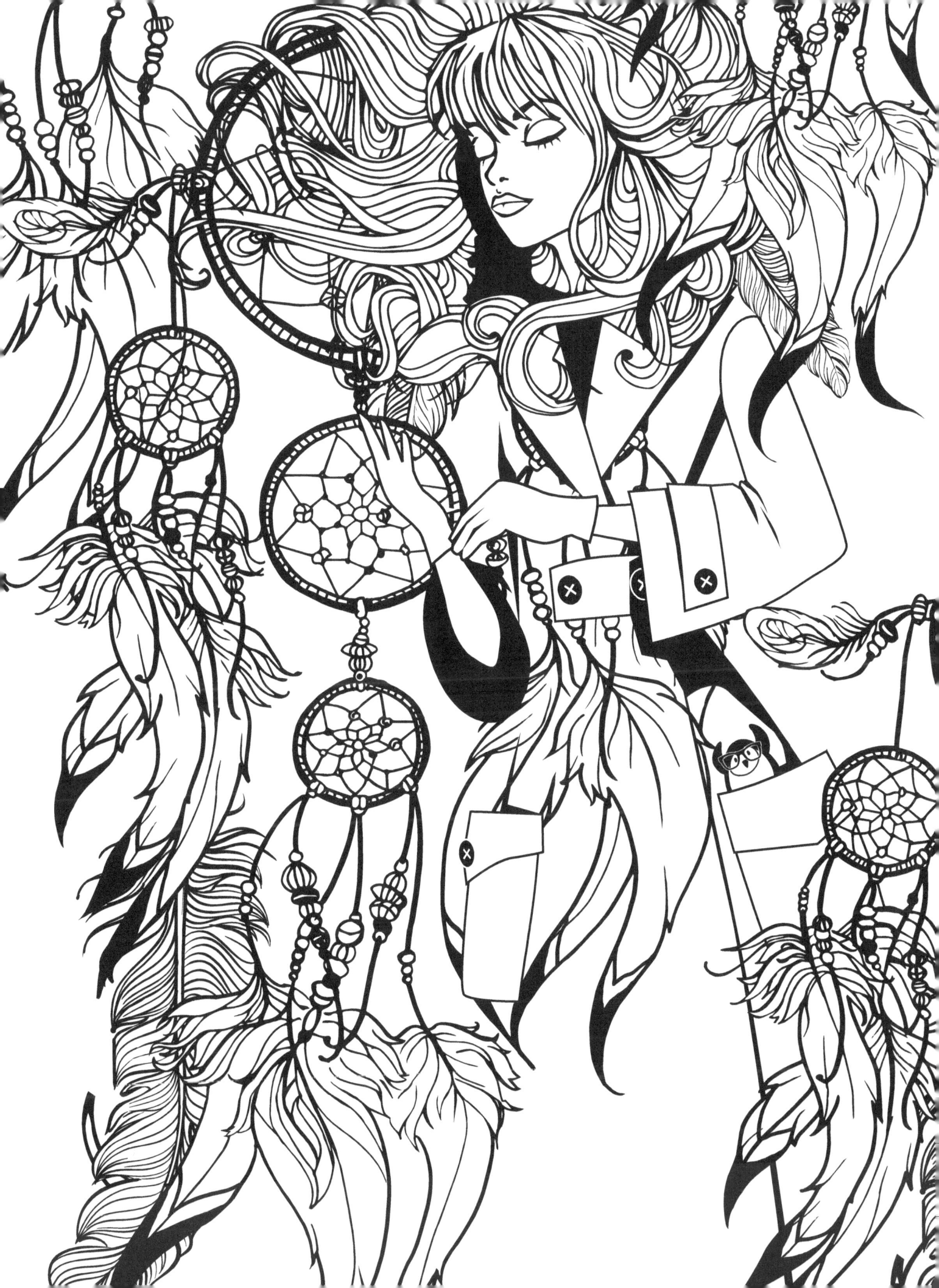

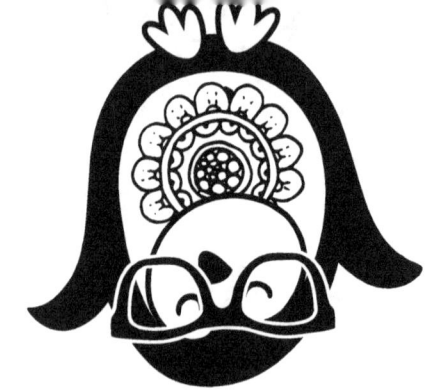

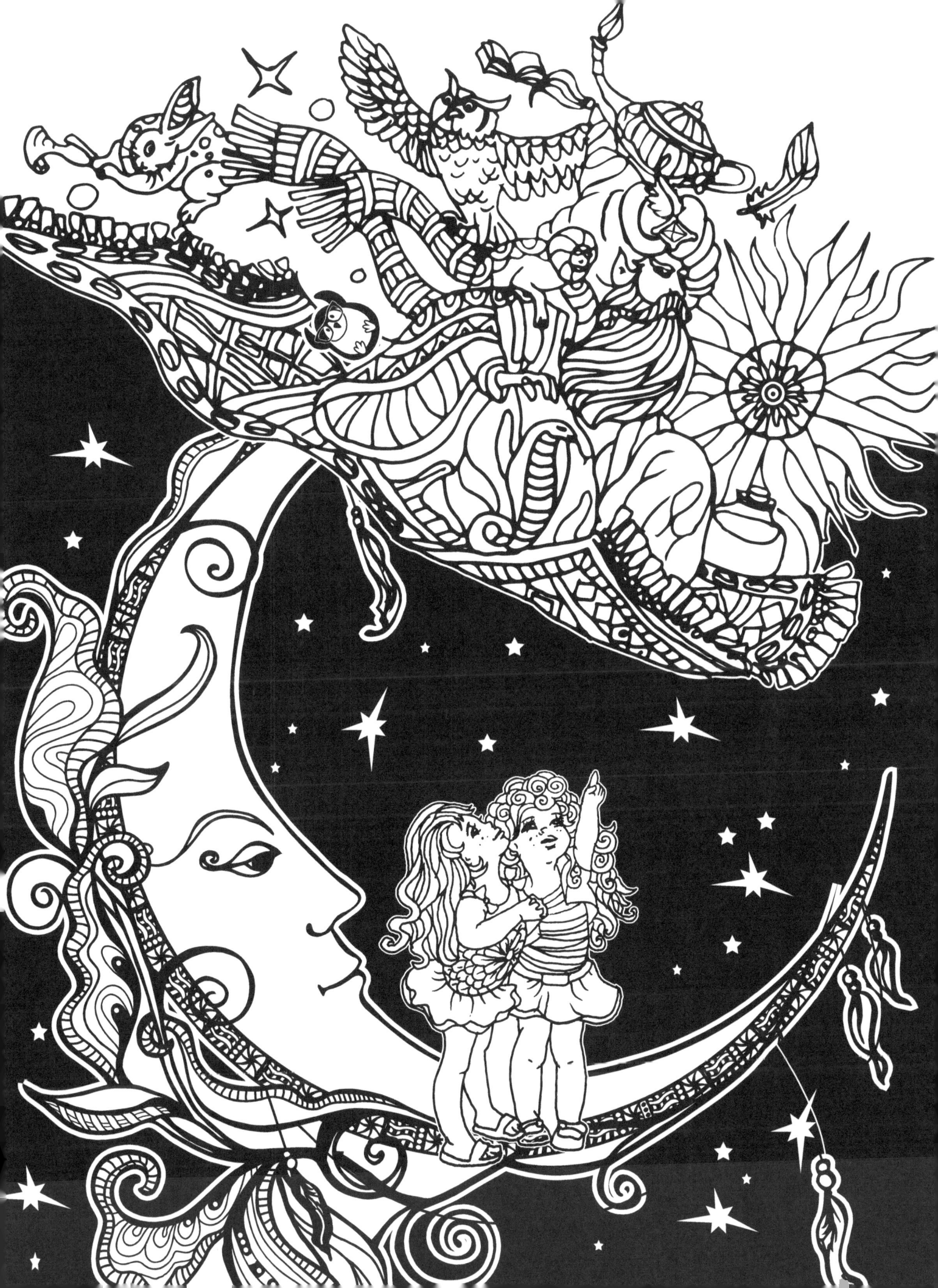

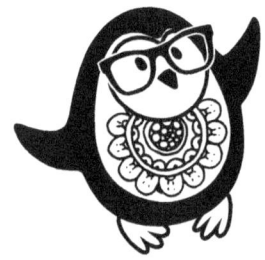

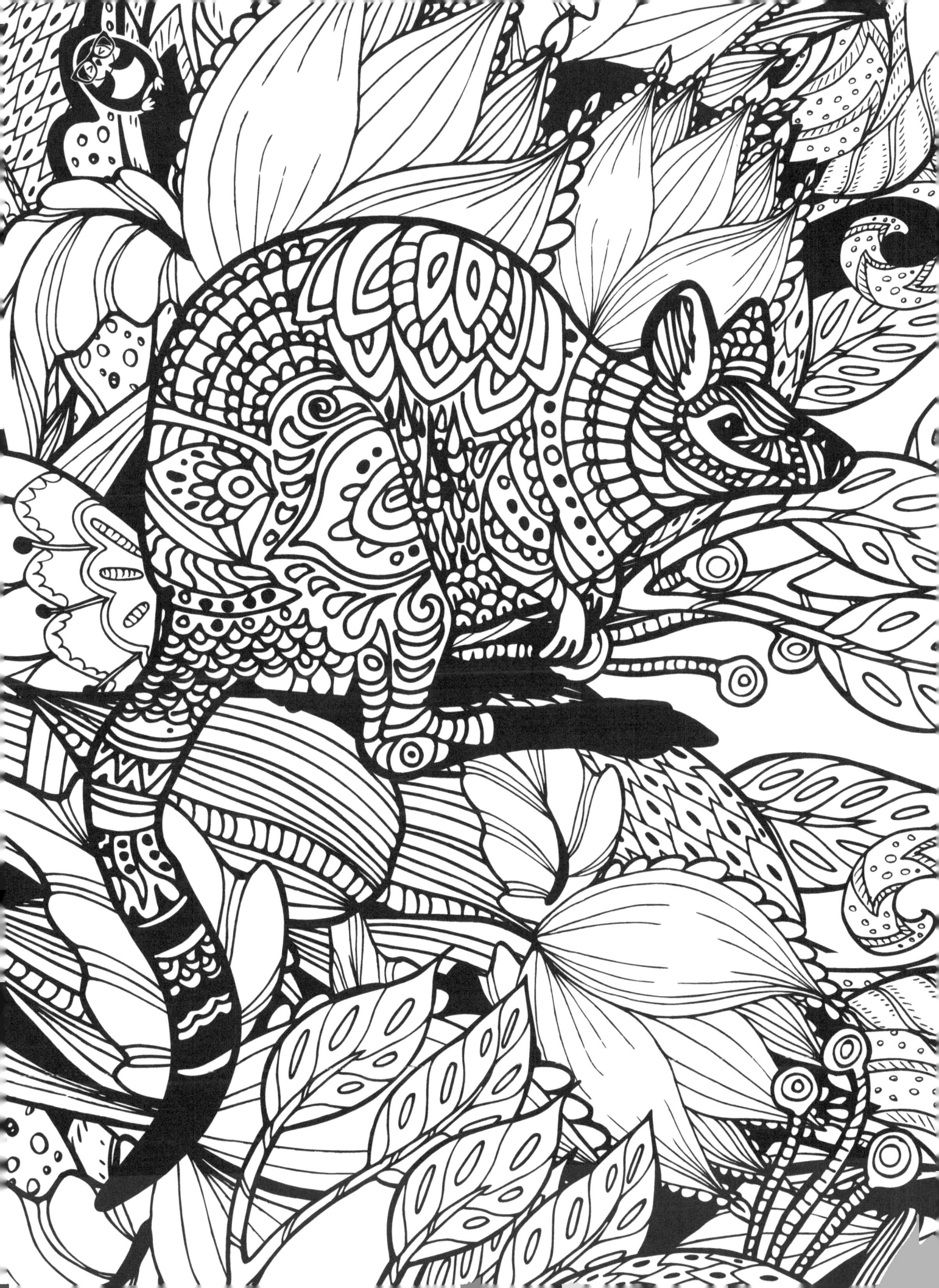

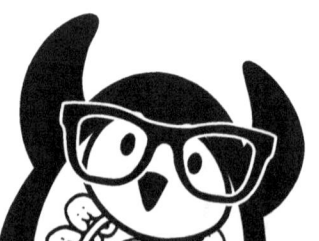

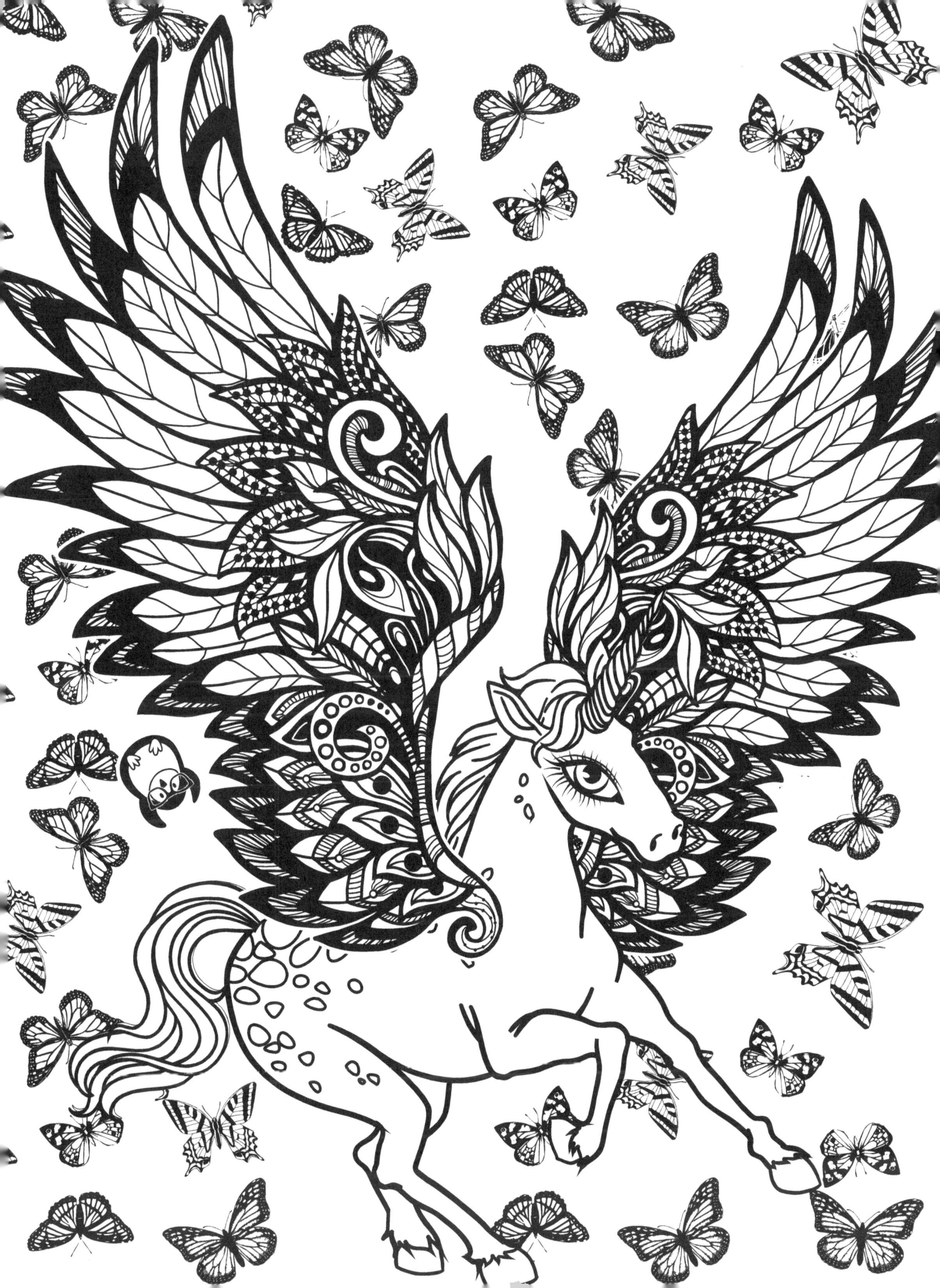

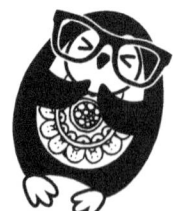

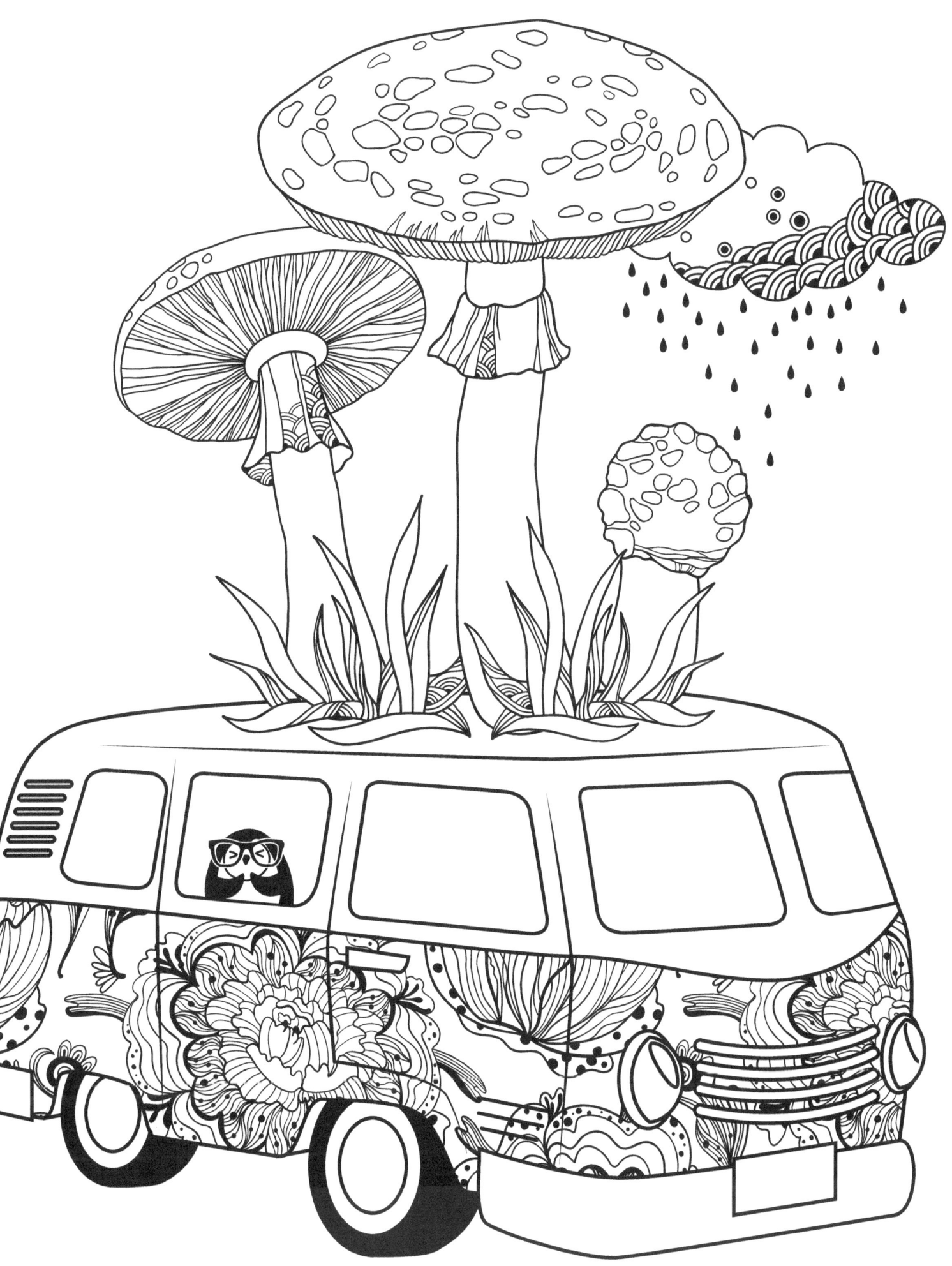

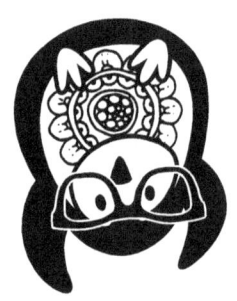

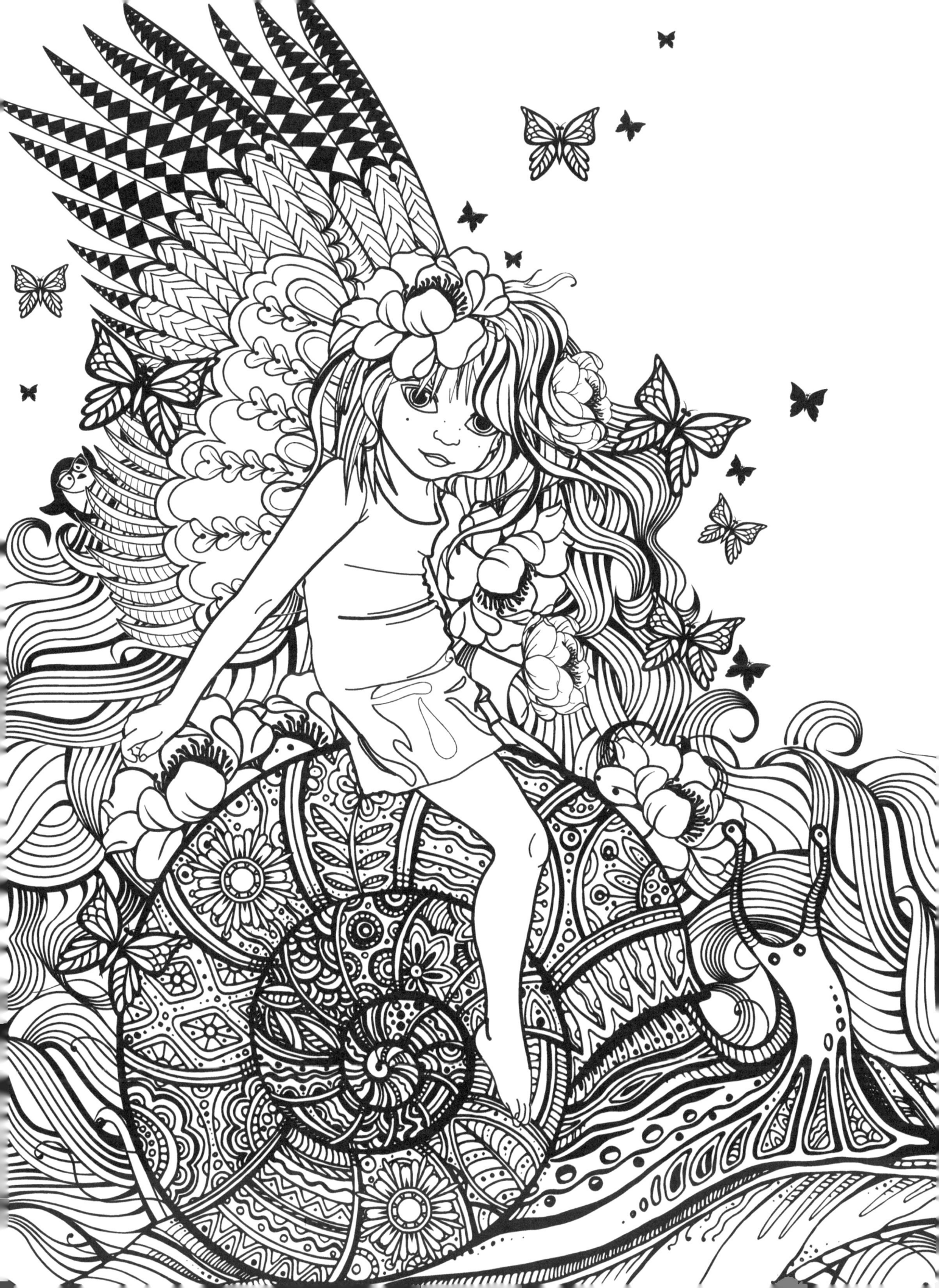

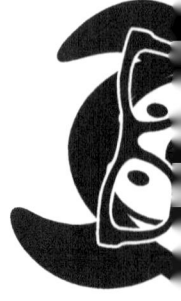

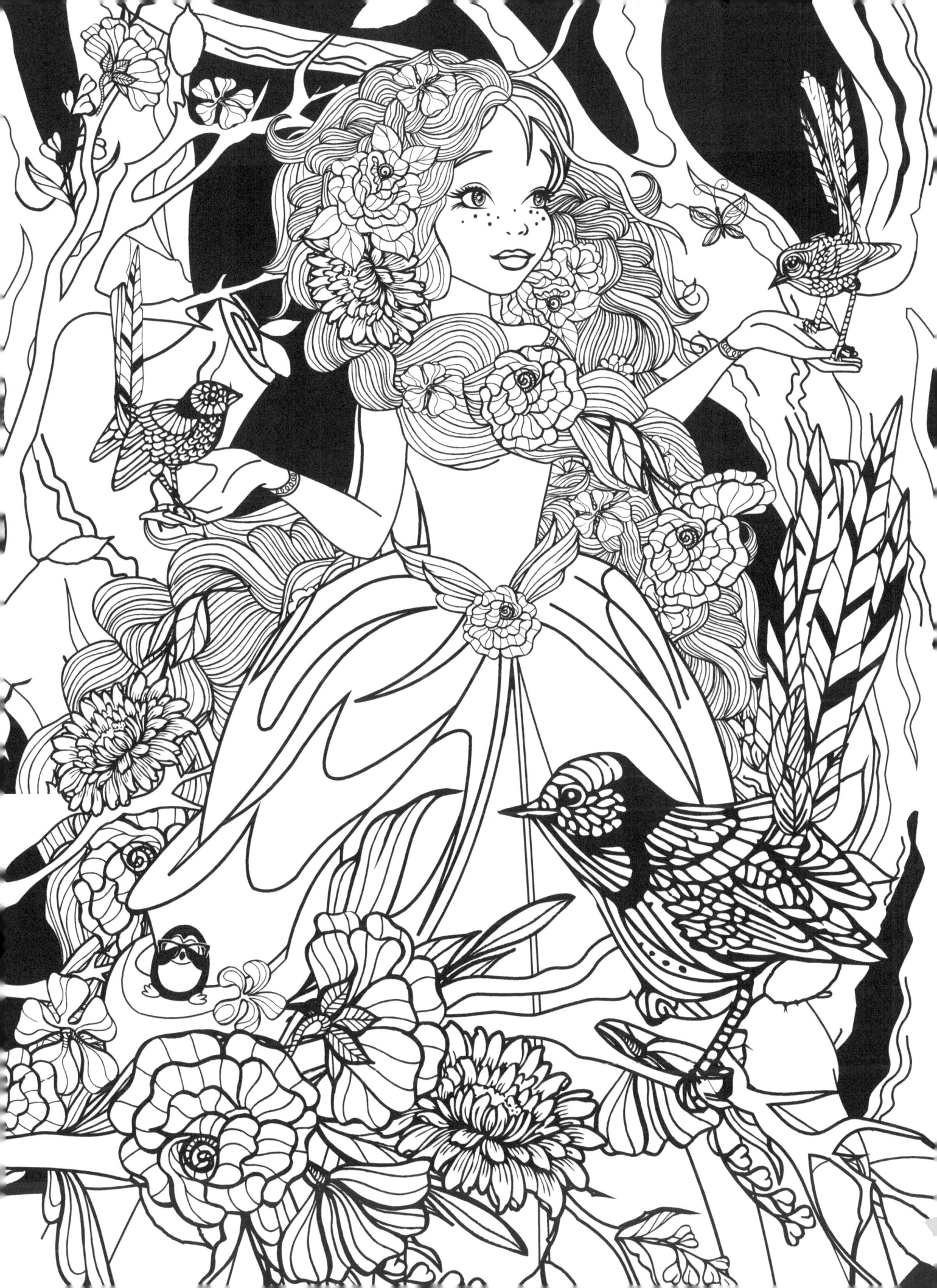

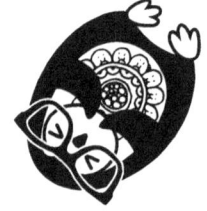

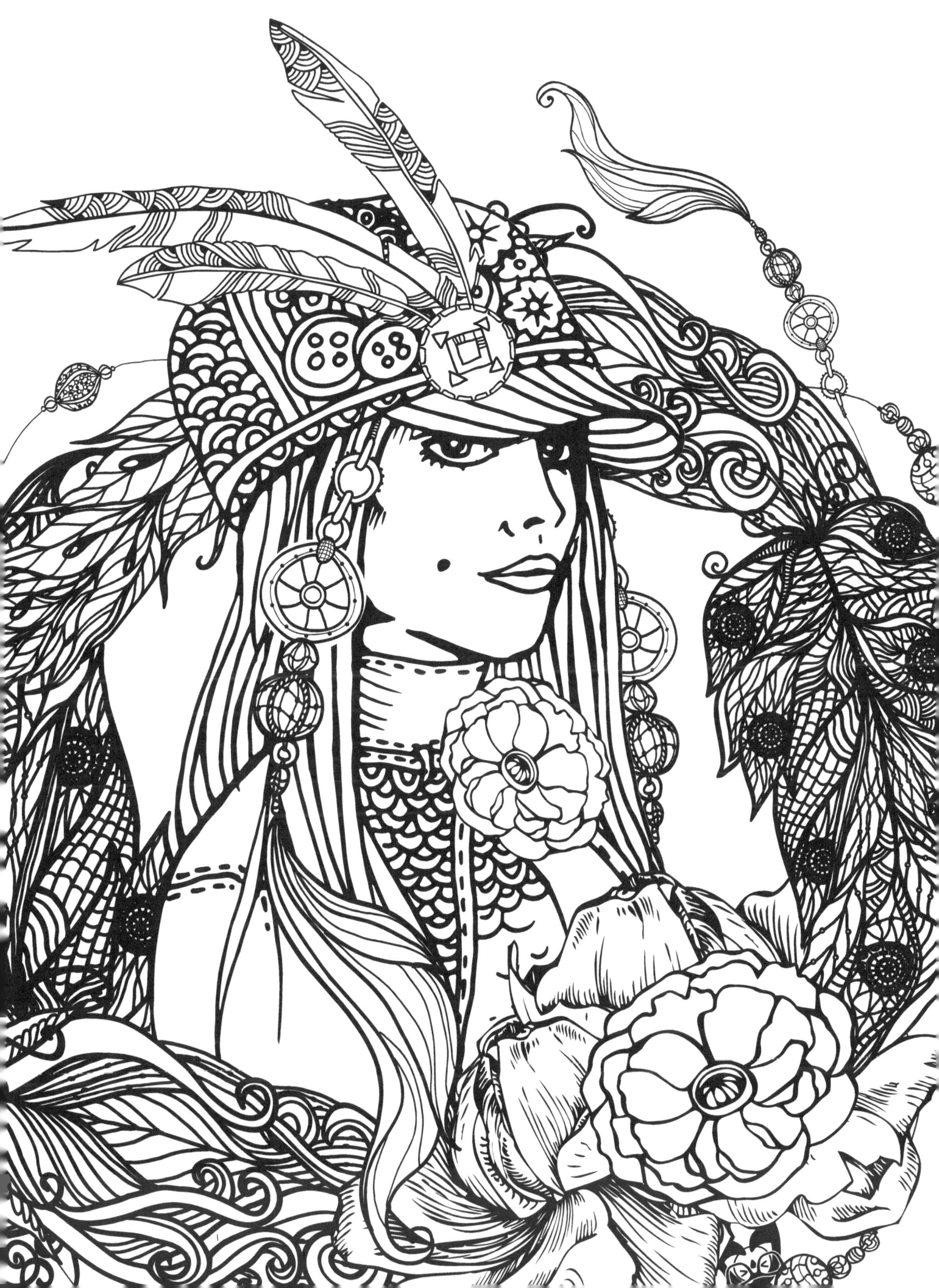

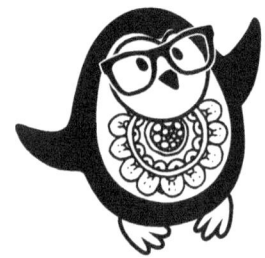

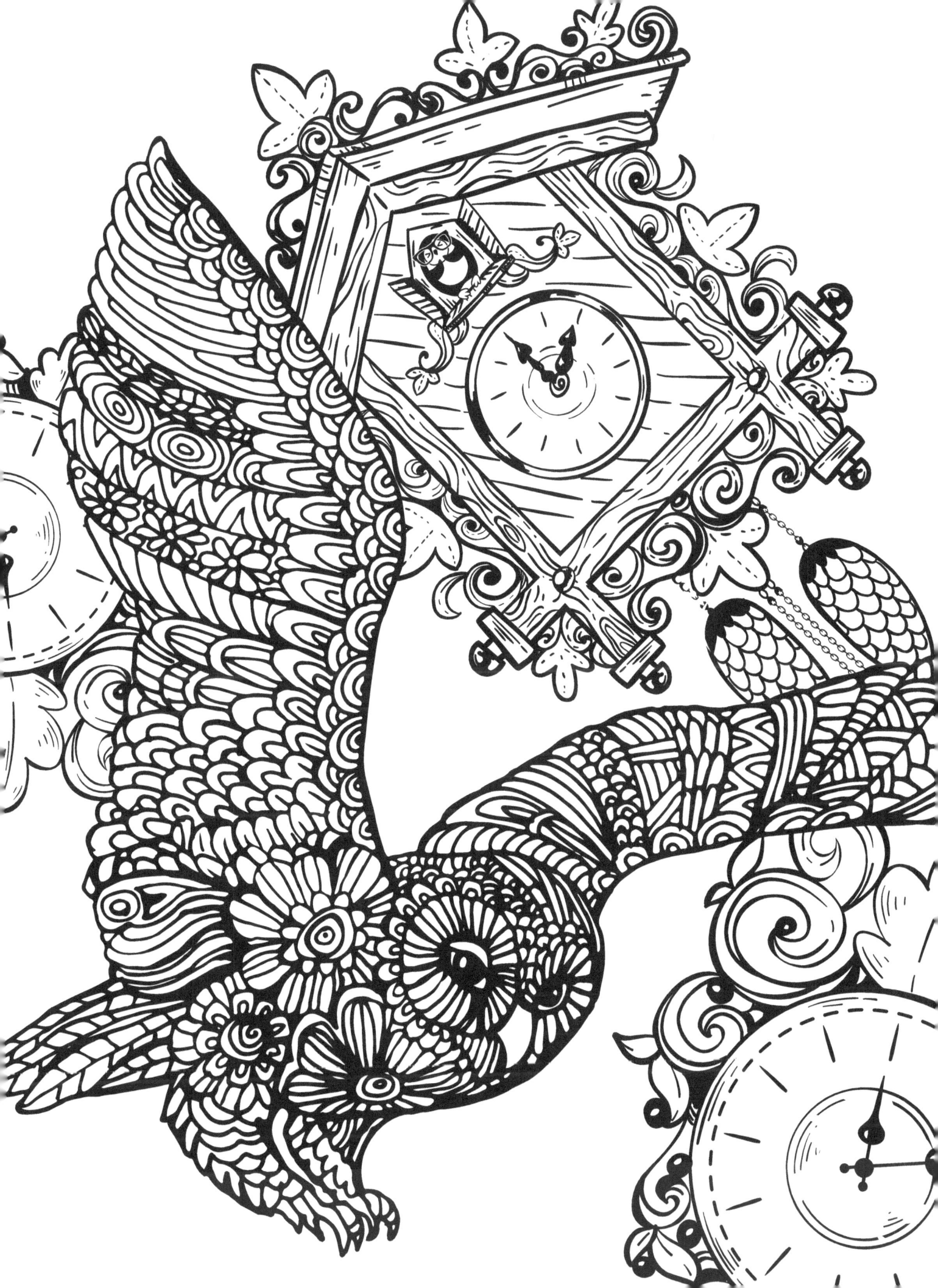

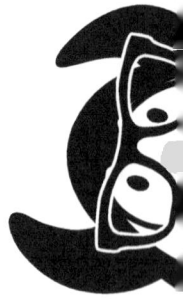

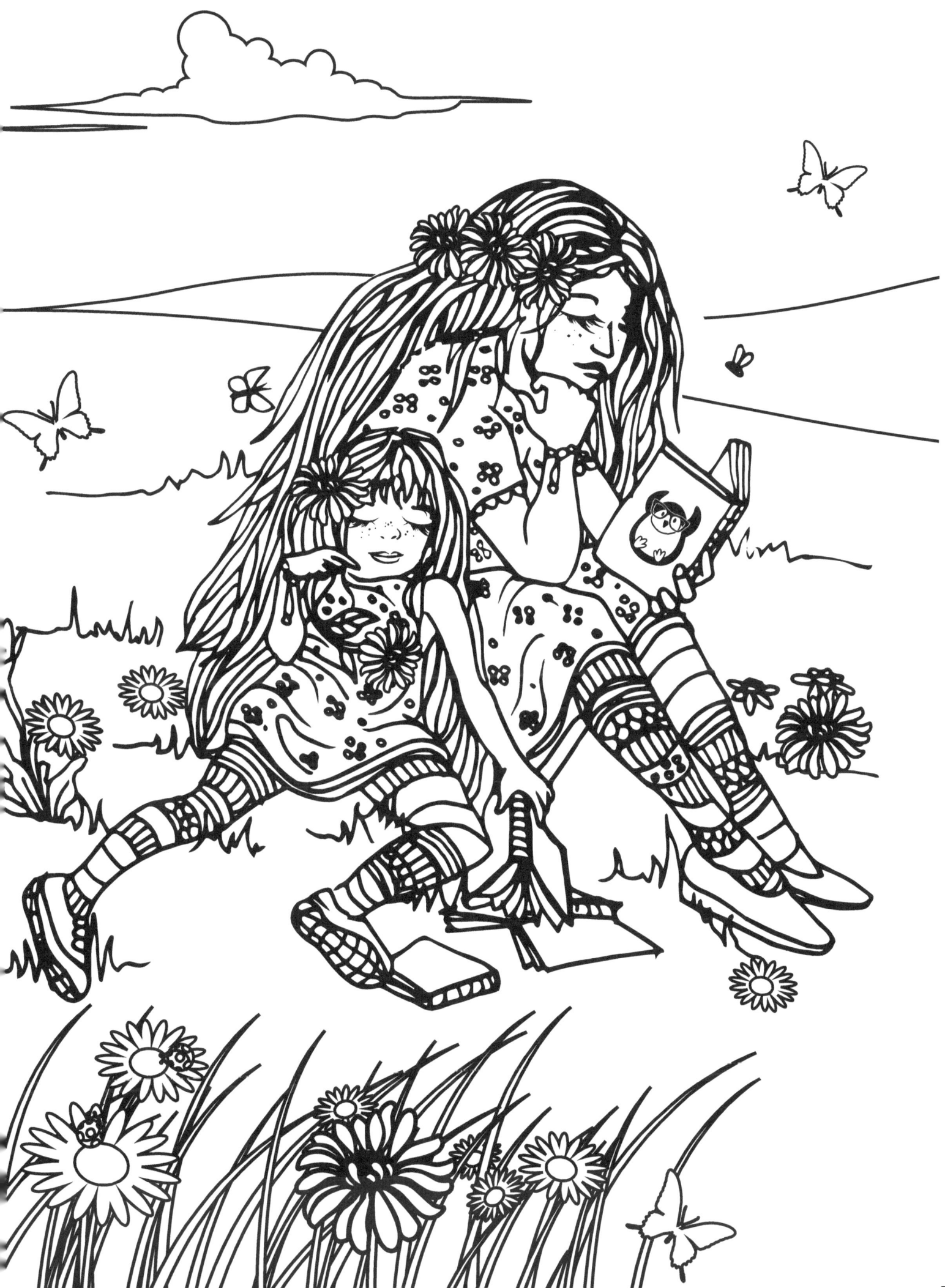

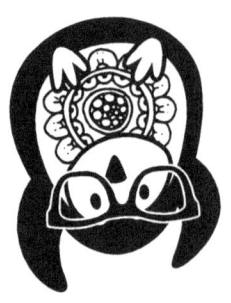

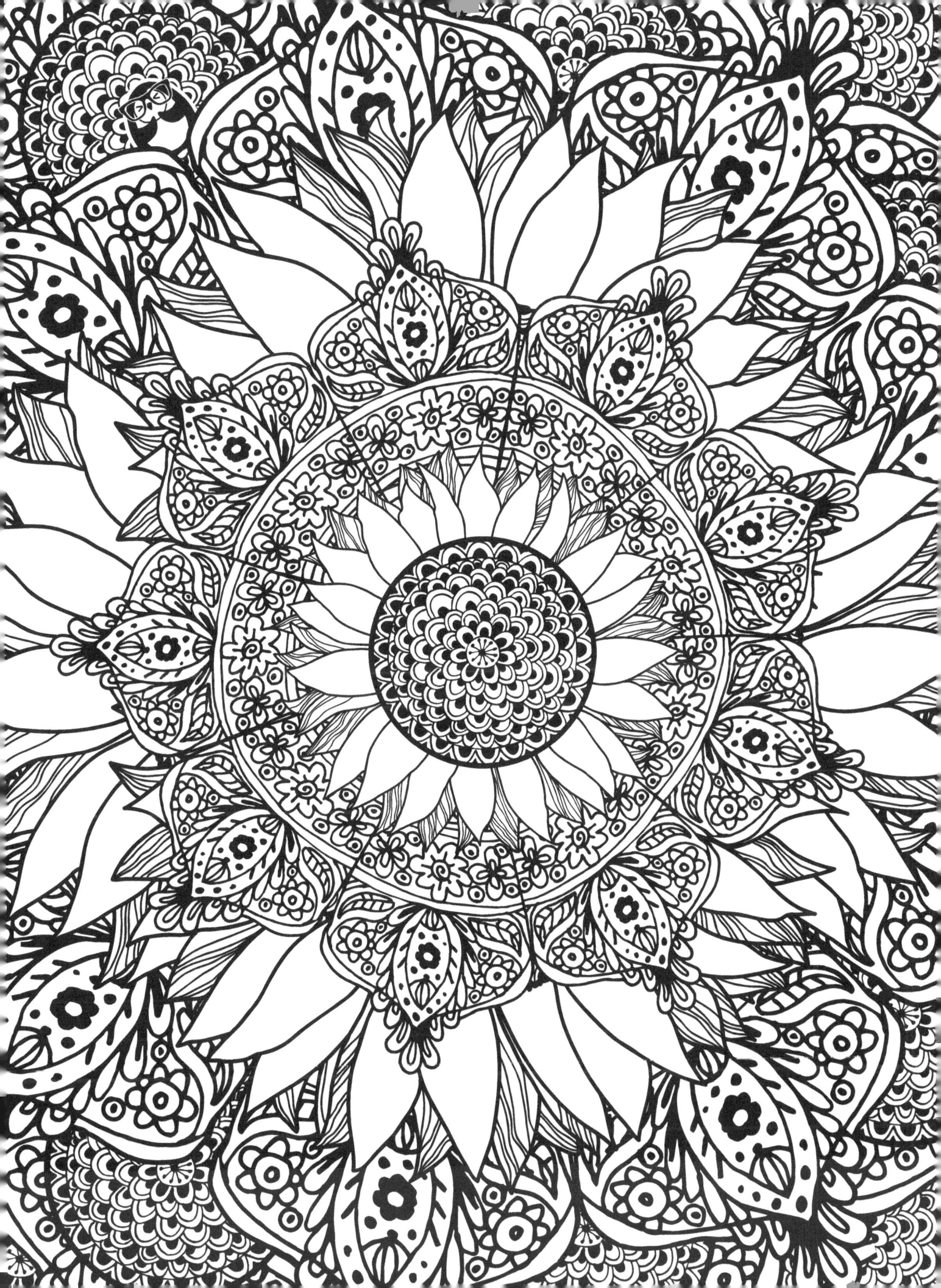

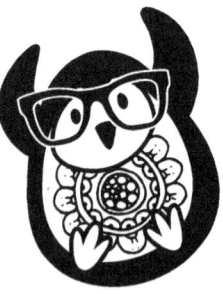

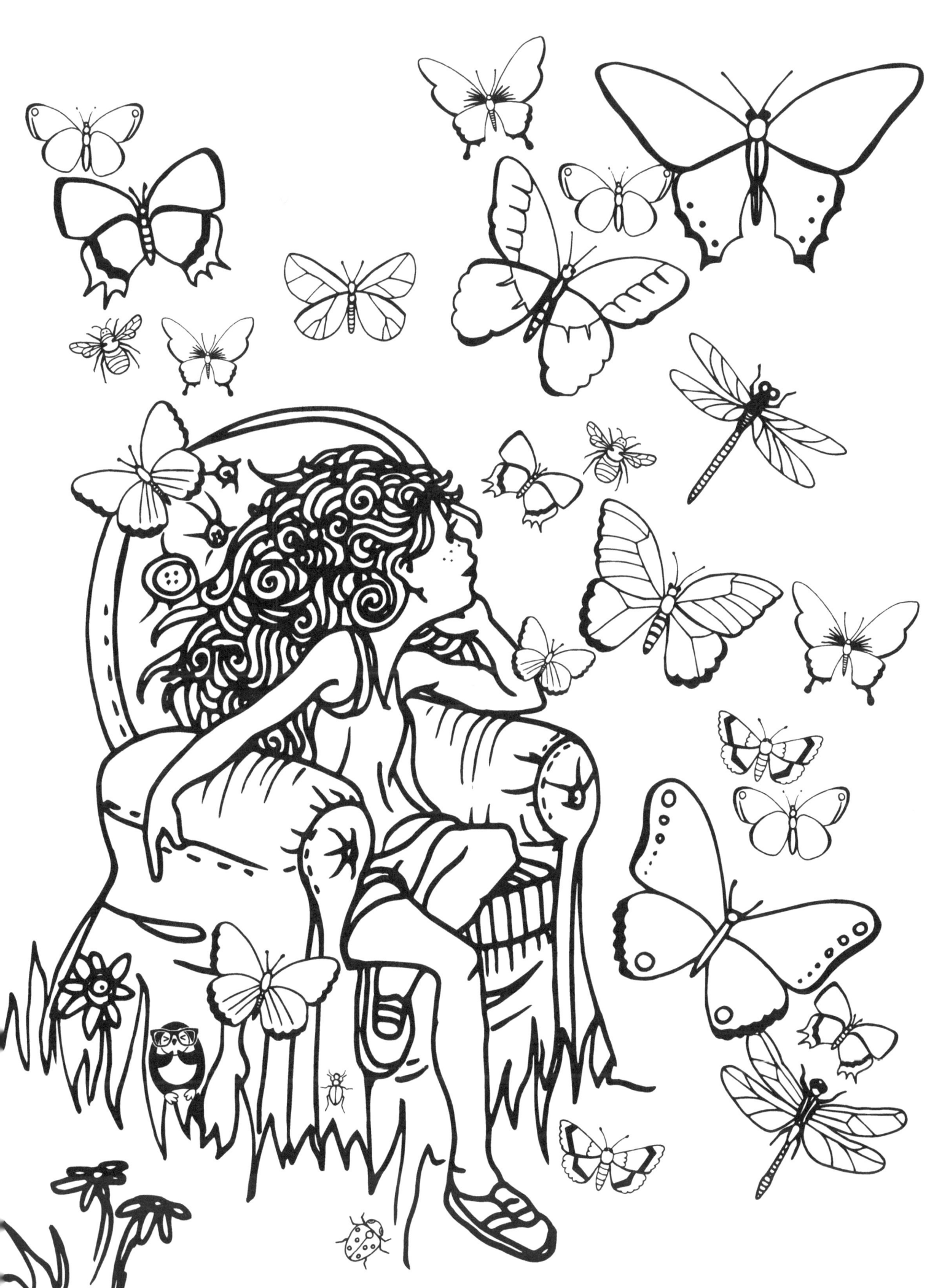

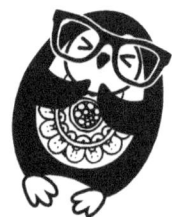

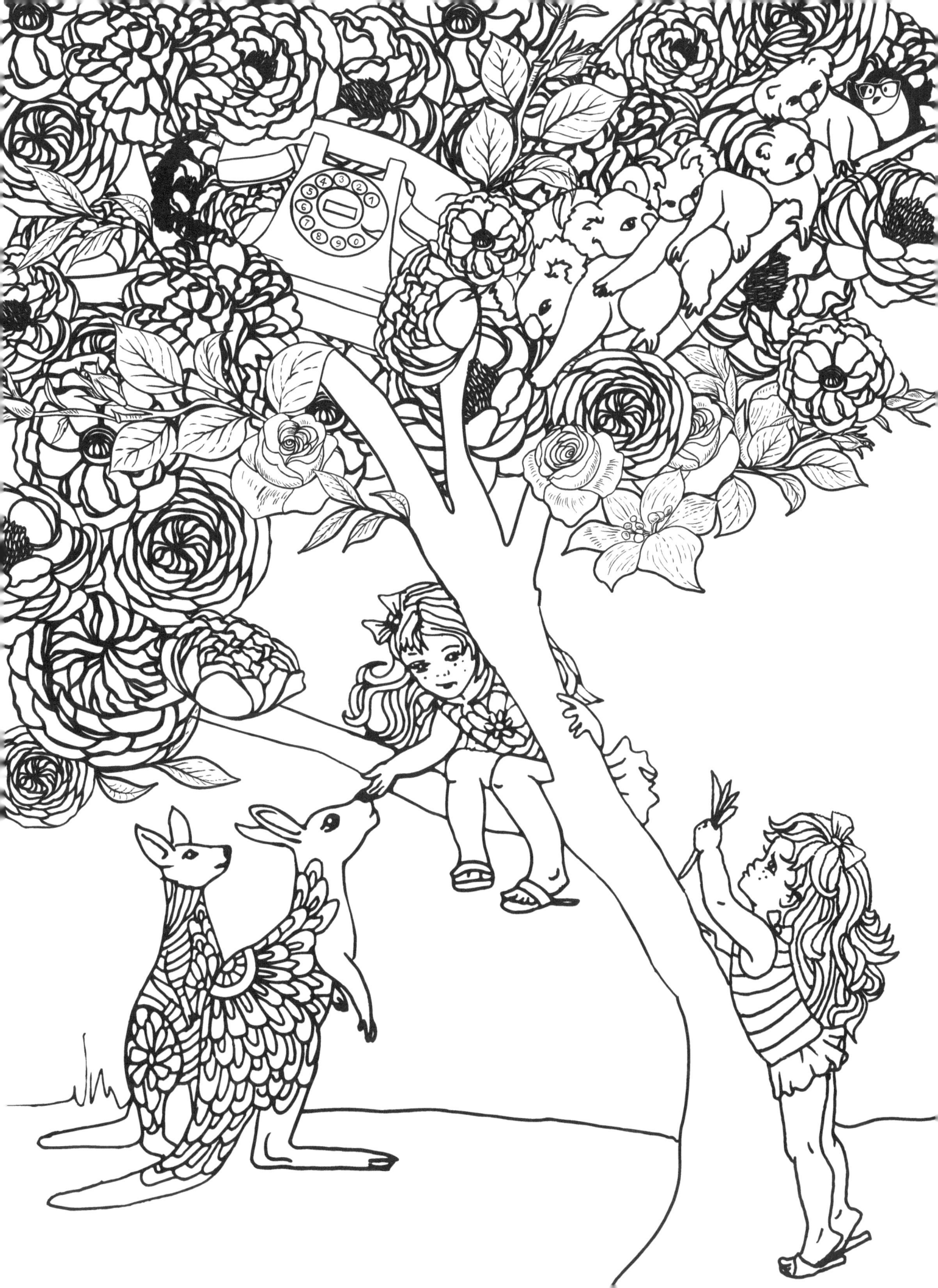

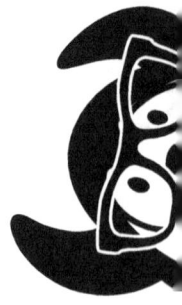

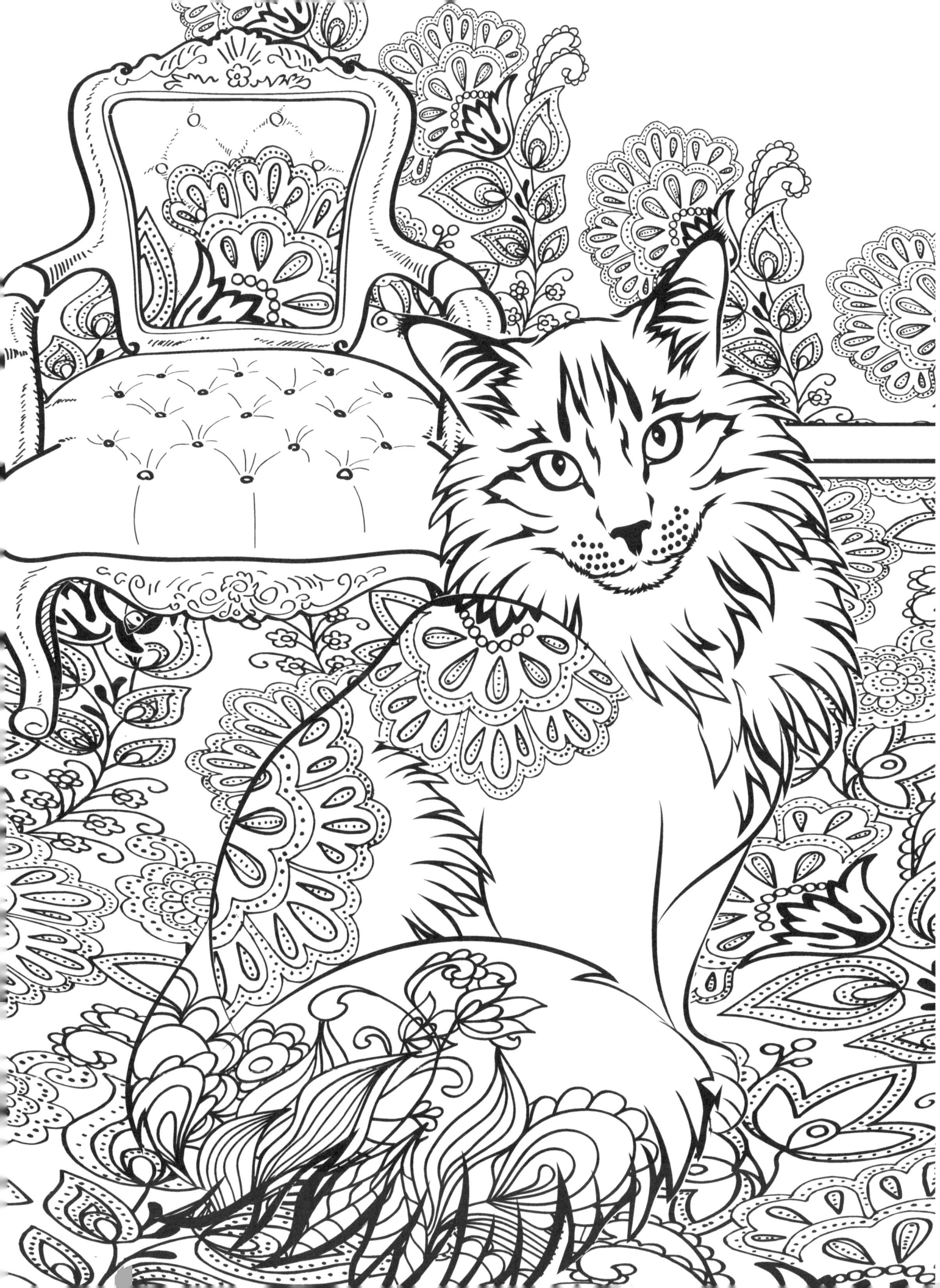

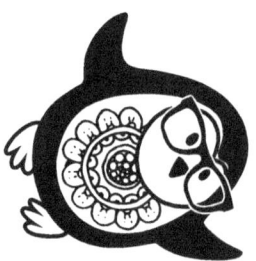

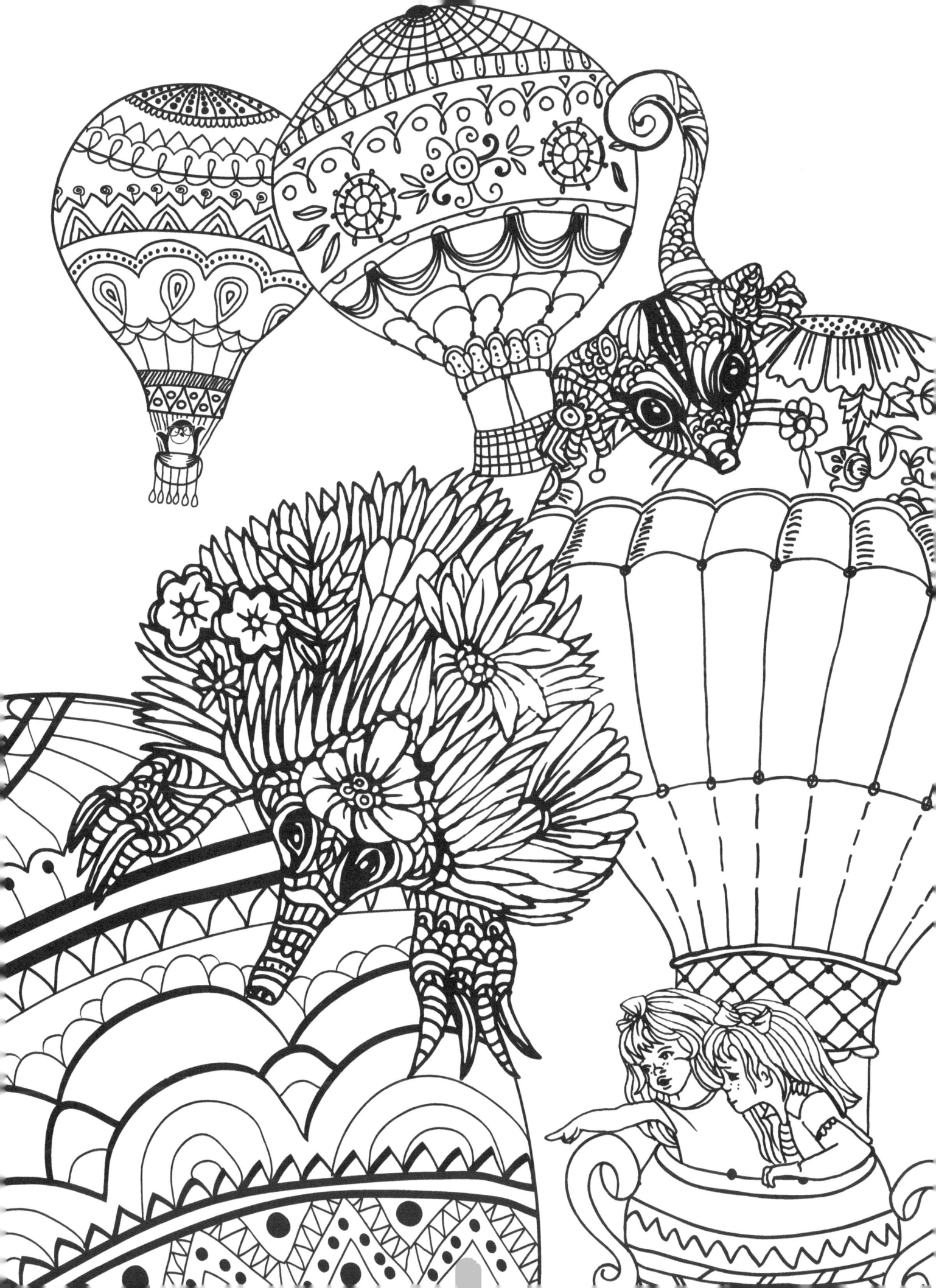

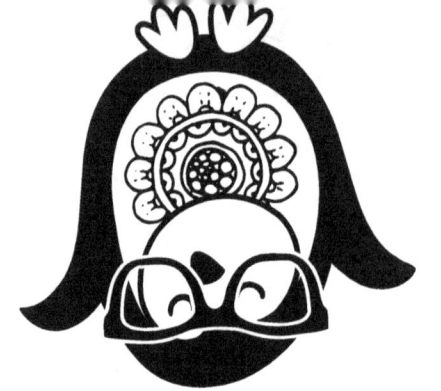

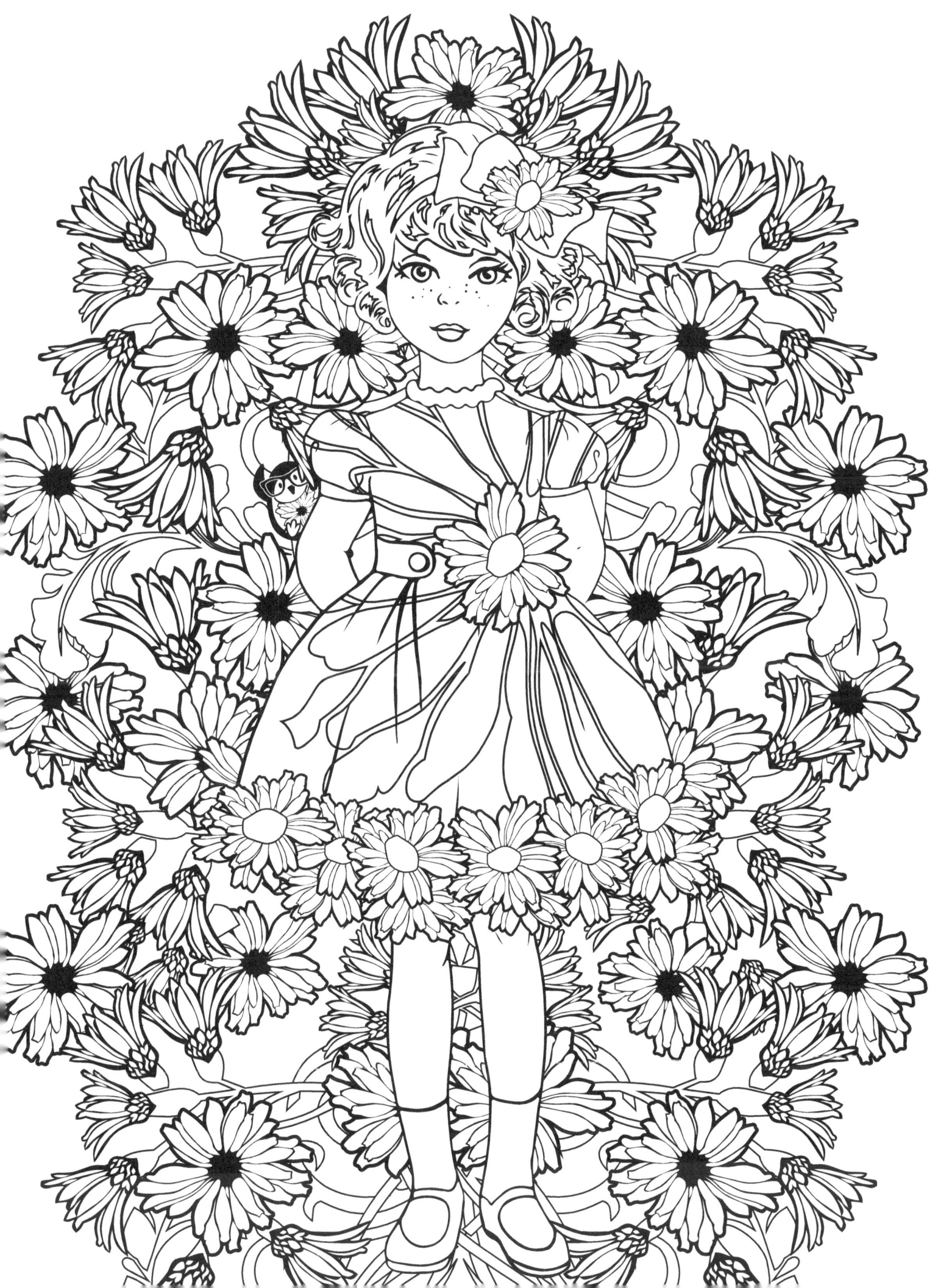

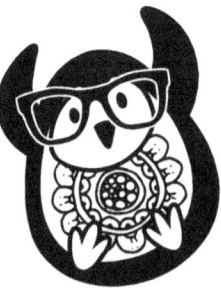

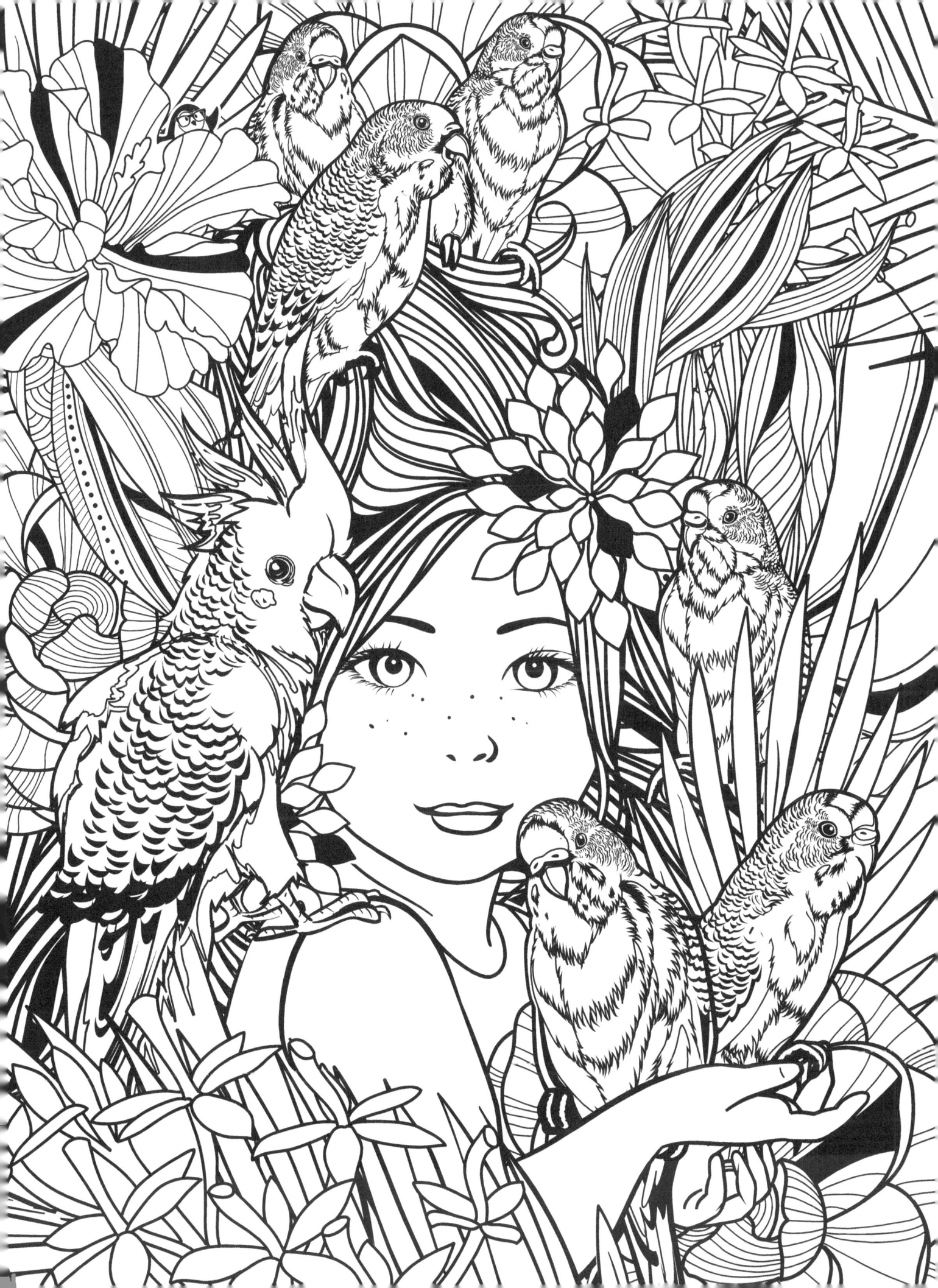

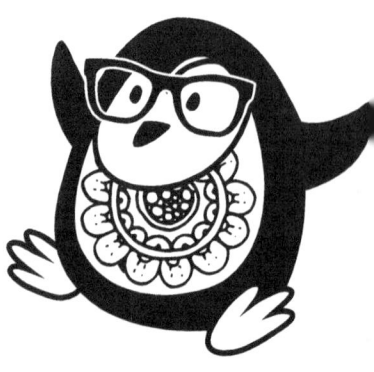

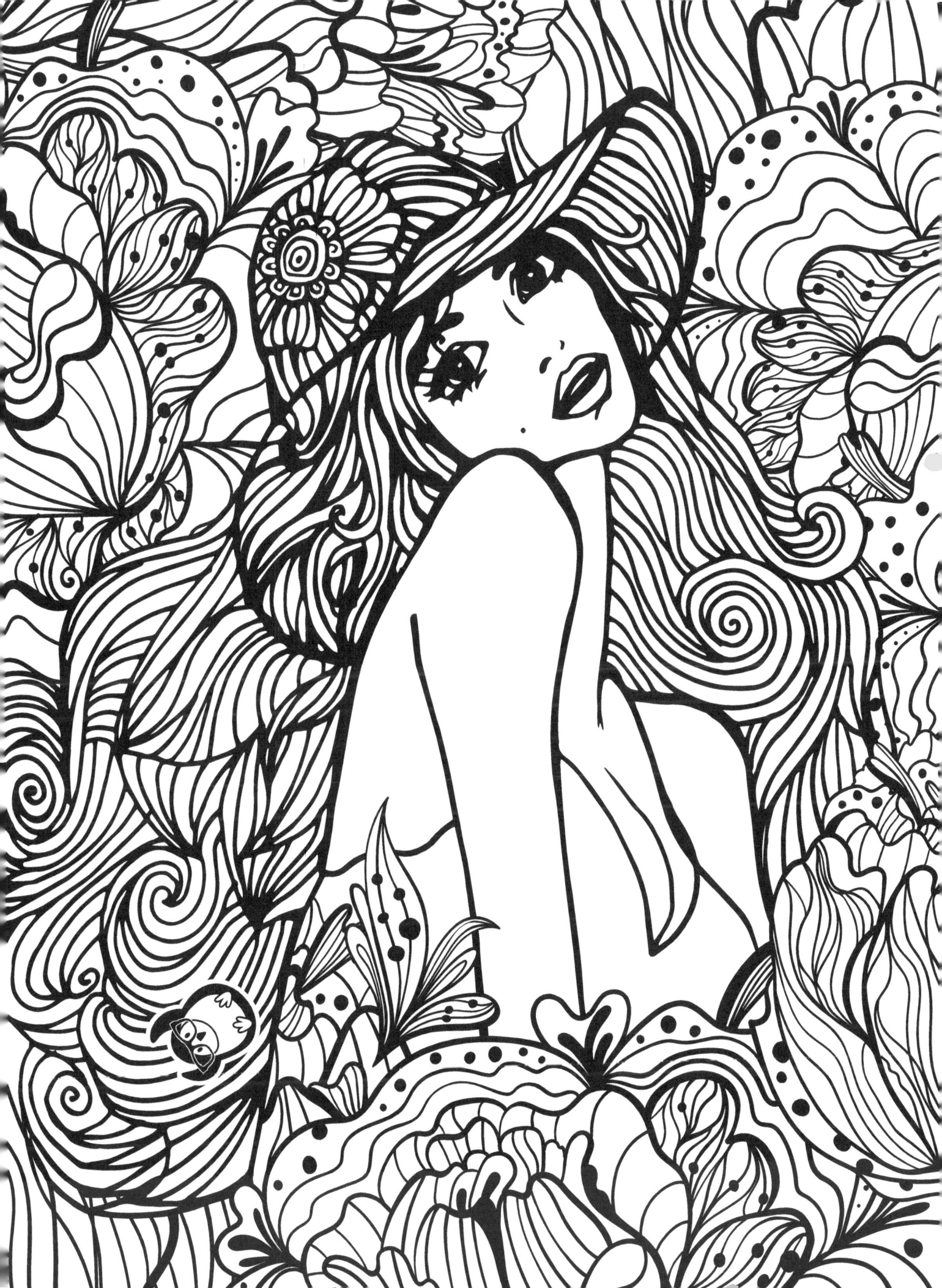

share your creations!

Find PERCY on Facebook:
www.facebook.com/percybooks

Follow us on Instagram:
@colourofcalm

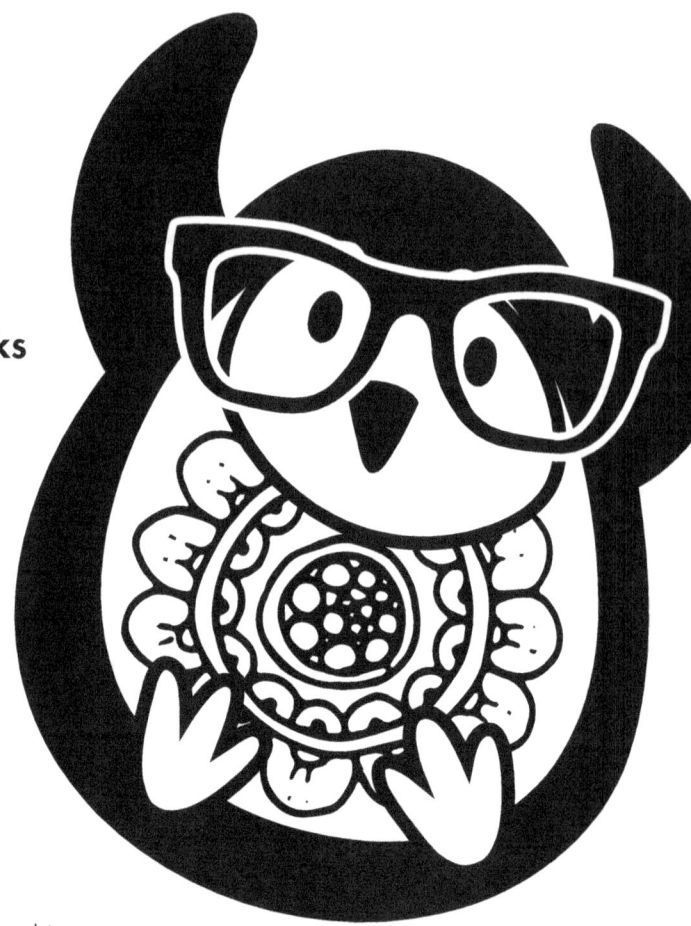

LOVE PERCY? Want More?

Find more PERCY colouring on our website:

www.colourofcalm.com.au

Worldwide Shipping Available on:

* Artist Edition Books (Spiral Bound Card Stock)

* Colouring Posters

* Colouring Greeting Cards and more!

Or find the full range of PERCY colouring books on Amazon

This Book is Dedicated to our three young daughters...

Ruby   *Milla*   *Sophie*

Designed & Illustrated in Australia

Cover art coloured in by 'Vermailene Barrios' and 'Narelle Craven'

www.ingramcontent.com/pod-product-compliance
Lightning Source LLC
Chambersburg PA
CBHW080647180526
45168CB00008B/3337